SUPERIOR TOUCH™

# BETTER THAN BOUILLON™
## CONCENTRATE

# WINNING RECIPES
# COOKBOOK

## Using Better Than Bouillon™
### *The Bouillon Made From Meat!*

*Superior Quality Foods, Inc.*

# Contents

# Acknowledgements

I am happy to be part of this very special cookbook put together by Superior Quality Foods. What makes this book unique is that most of the recipes have been provided by you, the Better Than Bouillon™ consumer, through national recipe contests sponsored by Melinda Lee's Food Shows. I had the pleasure of testing each recipe and found that they can be easily prepared in your home kitchen.

As you can tell from the various chapters in this book, Better Than Bouillon™ is versatile and enhances dishes from soups and stews to breads, rice, and pasta. Please note that the first chapter reflects recipes from the winners of Better Than Bouillon™ recipe contests. The balance of the recipes were submitted by Melinda Lee's radio listeners via Better Than Bouillon™ recipe contests. Superior Touch recipes were also added for a greater mix. If you have a favorite recipe using Better Than Bouillon™, send it to Superior Quality Foods. Who knows, perhaps it will be in the next edition of winning recipes!

Jorge Bruce, *Superior Touch Chef*

I am ecstatic to see such a great response to Superior Touch Better Than Bouillon™ from my radio show listeners. The level of participation in the Better Than Bouillon™ national recipe contests has been astounding! Without their involvement, this recipe collection would not be possible. I feel this is a testimony to the usefulness of Better Than Bouillon™: You just can't live without it in the kitchen. Thanks for participating and keep on cooking!

Melinda Lee, *Melinda Lee Food Shows*

# BETTER THAN BOUILLON™ Products

1  2  3

4  5  6

## BETTER THAN BOUILLON™ Products:

1  CHICKEN BASE
2  BEEF BASE
3  VEGETABLE BASE
4  CHILI BASE
5  CLAM BASE
6  LOBSTER BASE

# BETTER THAN BOUILLON™ History

*How "Better Than Bouillon™" Came to Be*

Meat bases have been a staple product in restaurants and food service kitchens for years. Consumer demand for reduced salt products led Superior Quality Foods to make its meat bases available as an alternative to salty bouillon cubes or canned broth. After much consumer testing and advice, Better Than Bouillon™ became the first product on the new Superior Touch consumer product line.

Better Than Bouillon™ is made from USDA-inspected meats. Unlike bouillon, meat is the first ingredient instead of salt. The superior Touch Better Than Bouillon™ product line has grown from the initial flavors of chicken and beef to include clam, lobster, vegetable, and a meatless chili base as well. If you haven't tried Better Than Bouillon™, you are in for a treat—it is the bouillon made from meat!

# Better Than Bouillon™
## Cooking Tips

Following are helpful hints and tips for cooking with Better Than Bouillon™ products.

*Instead of salt:* Substitute 1 Tbs Better Than Bouillon™ for 1 tsp salt.

*For boiling rice, pasta, potatoes, or any vegetable:* Add 1 tsp Better Than Bouillon™ per cup of boiling water.

*For poaching or steaming fish:* Add 1 tsp Better Than Bouillon™ per cup of poaching or steaming water.

*For steaming vegetables:* Add 1 tsp Better Than Bouillon™ per cup of steaming water.

*For reduced-fat wok cooking:* Substitute ratio of 2 tsp Better Than Bouillon™ per cup water for the oil.

*For simple gravies:* Make a roux of 2 Tbs flour and 2 Tbs butter; add 2 cups broth (2 tsp Better Than Bouillon™ Base dissolved in 2 cups hot water). Add meat juices if available. Season with pepper to taste.

*As an extender for au jus:* Add 2 tsp Better Than Bouillon™ Beef Base dissolved in 1 cup hot water to 1 cup au jus from roasting.

*For a magnificent homestyle meatloaf:* Add 1 rounded tsp Better Than Bouillon™ Beef Base for each pound of your favorite meatloaf recipe. Simply dissolve Better Than Bouillon™ Beef Base into the egg mixture during preparation. Note: Better Than Bouillon™ replaces the salt!

*For world champion chicken patties and chicken balls:* Add 1 rounded tsp Better Than Bouillon™ Chicken Base to each pound of your outdoor bar-becue chicken burgers or Italian chicken meatballs. Dissolve Better Than Bouillon™ Chicken Base into the water and egg mixture during preparation. Note: Better Than Bouillon™ replaces the salt!

*For scrumptious scrambled eggs and outstanding omelettes:*  Add 1/4 tsp Better Than Bouillon™ Chicken Base for every 2 eggs when preparing scrambled eggs or omelettes.  Note:  Better Than Bouillon™ is a salt replacement!

*For an out-of-the-ordinary oriental stir-fry:*  Dissolve 1/2 tsp Better Than Bouillon™ Chicken Base in 3/4 cup water and add to your favorite stir-fry.  Use a 50/50 cornstarch and water mixture to create a delicious, healthful sauce.

*For mouth-watering mashed potatoes:*  Add 2 tsp Better Than Bouillon™ Chicken Base for every 3 pounds of potatoes to the milk or cream before whipping into potatoes.

*For bodacious baked beans:*  Add 1/4 tsp Better Than Bouillon™ Beef Base to your favorite baked bean recipe or prepared canned beans instead of salt.

*For simple savory stuffing:*  Add 1 rounded tsp Better Than Bouillon™ Chicken or Beef Base to your traditional homestyle stuffing recipe to add great chicken or beef flavor without having to bake the stuffing inside of the bird or around the roast!

*For fabulous french fries:*  Soak raw, sliced potatoes in 2 Tbs Better Than Bouillon™ Beef Base dissolved in 2 qts chilled water overnight.  Be sure to dry potatoes thoroughly before frying.

*For miraculous marinades:*  Add 2 tsp Better Than Bouillon™ Beef or Chicken Base to each cup of your favorite marinade recipe.

*For the best barbecue sauce:*  Add 1/4 to 3/4 tsp Better Than Bouillon™ Beef or Chicken Base to 1/2 cup of your favorite prepared barbecue sauce.

# WINNING RECIPES

$\mathcal{R}$ecipes featured in this chapter reflect the top recipes selected from those submitted for two contests held on Melinda Lee's Food Shows. Melinda, her staff, and representatives from Better Than Bouillon™ prepared, tested, and tasted each recipe and then assigned it a score based on flavor, presentation, and ease of preparation.

$\mathcal{E}$njoy these recipes and relish in their use of Better Than Bouillon™ as a flavor enhancement or alternative to salt. The recipes are simple to prepare, and show just how easy it is to adapt your own favorite recipes with Better Than Bouillon™.

# GINGER APPLE BEEF

**Sheila Meyers Cavazos**

*Use Beef Base*
*Servings: 4*

*2 cups thinly sliced beef*
*1 Tbs vegetable oil*
*1 bell pepper, sliced*
*1/2 onion, sliced*
*2 small red apples, sliced*
*1/2 cup Chinese pea pods*
*Fresh parsley, chopped*

### S A U C E

*1 tsp sweet and sour sauce*
*2 1/2 tsp Better Than*
    *Bouillon™ Beef Base*
    *dissolved in*
    *2 1/2 cups hot water*
*1 tsp minced fresh ginger*
*1/8 tsp pepper*

*1 Tbs cornstarch dissolved in*
    *1 Tbs cold water*

Combine all sauce ingredients and set aside.

Marinate beef in 2 Tbs sauce at least one hour.

Heat oil and lightly sauté marinated beef. Add peppers and onions and sauté just until vegetables are glazed. Stir in remaining sauce. Heat to just boiling; add cornstarch mixture to thicken. Add apples and immediately remove from heat. Garnish with pea pods and parsley, and serve with rice (recipe page vii).

# BETTER THAN PASTA
# PASTA SAUCE
*Use Chicken Base*
Vada Kehrer and Vanessa Scherry
*Servings: 8*

*2 Tbs butter*
*2 cloves garlic, chopped*
*1 large Vidalia onion,*
*chopped*
*3 medium tomatoes, chopped*
*1/8 cup lemon juice*
*1/8 cup dry white wine*
*2 tsp oregano*
*1 Tbs fresh sweet basil*
*1/4 cup fresh grated parme-*
*san cheese*
*1 Tbs Better Than Bouillon™*
*Chicken Base*
*1/2 cup tomato sauce*
*1 lb pasta of your choice*

Heat medium skillet on medium high. Add butter, garlic, and onion in pan and sauté until tender. Add tomatoes, lemon juice, and white wine; cook down. Add oregano, basil, and parmesan cheese and simmer.

In separate bowl, combine Better Than Bouillon™ Chicken Base and tomato sauce. Add to skillet and simmer on low for 5 minutes. Toss with pasta and serve.

# ARBOR HARVEST LAMBOREE
Judith O. O. Toubes
*Use Vegetable Base*
*Servings: 6*

*6 sirloin lamb chops, 1-inch*
*thick, 6 oz each*
*1/4 tsp pepper*
*3 Tbs unsweetened cocoa*
*1 tsp Better Than Bouillon™*
*Vegetable Base*
*1 cup boiling apple juice*
*1 1/2 tsp ground oregano*
*6 slices fresh tomato*
*12 sprigs fresh parsley*

Remove visible fat from lamb chops. Combine pepper, cocoa, Better Than Bouillon™ Vegetable Base, boiling apple juice, and oregano. Dip lamb chops in mixture and broil for 12 minutes, 6 minutes on each side. Baste with cocoa mixture after turning and before serving. Serve immediately, topped with tomato slice and two sprigs of parsley.

# PORK IN THICK CHILE SAUCE
**Francisco Calderon**

## S A U C E

5–6 tomatillos
3–4 dry chilies, washed,
    stems and seeds
    removed (chile guajillo
    for a medium hot sauce,
    chile mulato for a
    medium-to-hot sauce,
    New Mexico chile for
    a hot sauce)
3 cups water
2–3 cloves garlic
1–2 Tbs Better Than
    Bouillon™ Chicken Base

1 1/2 lbs pork sirloin, cubed
3 Tbs canola oil

1 large onion, sliced
Lemon
Corn tortillas

Boil tomatillos (outer skin removed) and chilies in water for 20 minutes until chilies are tender. Blend chilies, tomatillos, and garlic in food processor or blender with 2 cups of water from the pan until smooth. Consistency should be somewhat thin. Add 1 Tbs Better Than Bouillon™ Chicken Base and blend until smooth. Taste and add more Better Than Bouillon™ Chicken Base if needed. Set aside.

Sauté pork in canola oil until pork is well-cooked and well-browned. While meat and oil are still hot, pour chile sauce over meat and sauté over medium heat for about 5 minutes, stirring continuously. Reduce heat to low and cook an additional 5 minutes to let skin form on top of mixture. Stir again (sauce should be thick). Remove from heat and serve with raw onions, lemon, and steamed corn tortillas.

# PICADA STEW

**Dennis Simanaitis**

*Use Chicken Base*
*Servings: 4*

2 Tbs extra virgin olive oil
1/2 lb low-fat turkey
   sausage, sliced in
   1/2-inch pieces
1/4 tsp paprika
1 red onion, coarsely
   chopped
1/2 cup fresh green beans,
   ends snipped, cut into
   1-inch pieces
2 Tbs Better Than Bouillon™
   Chicken Base dissolved
   in 6 cups water
Better Than Bouillon™
   Chicken Base, to taste
3 tomatoes, peeled, seeded,
   and coarsely chopped
1/2 cup frozen crowder peas
   or black-eyed peas
2 turnips, peeled and coarsely chopped
1/3 cup uncooked pasta
   (penne or macaroni
   work well)

## P I C A D A

3 cloves garlic, diced
1/4 cup chopped parsley or
   cilantro
3 Tbs pine nuts, toasted
2 Tbs grated parmesan
   cheese
1-2 Tbs extra virgin olive oil,
   to moisten

Heat olive oil on low/moderate heat in Dutch oven. Add sausage, paprika and onion. Sauté until sausage is lightly browned and onion is translucent. Add green beans and toss lightly. Add Better Than Bouillon™ Chicken Broth. Heat to a fast simmer, just short of boiling. Lower heat to lowest simmer for 5–7 minutes. Taste, and add more Better Than Bouillon™ Chicken Base, if needed. Add tomatoes, crowder peas and turnips. If using dried pasta, add and cook for 6–8 minutes; if using fresh pasta, delay to allow for faster cooking time. Remove from heat.

To make picada, crush together garlic, parsley, toasted pine nuts and parmesan cheese. Moisten with olive oil to make a thick paste. A mortar and pestle make a more authentic paste, but a food processor may be substituted. Add the picada to the stew. Blend and simmer until well-heated. Serve with salad and crusty bread.

# GINGERY ROOT VEGETABLE SOUP

**Barbara M. Dickinson**

*Use Chicken Base*
*Yield: approx. one gallon*
*Servings: 10–12*

3 Tbs Better Than Bouillon™
  Chicken Base
8 cups water
2 lbs carrots, peeled and
  coarsely chopped
1 medium onion, coarsely
  chopped
2 medium potatoes, peeled
  and coarsely chopped
1 butternut squash, cooked,
  cooled and peeled
2–3 stems fresh parsley,
  chopped
1 bay leaf
1/2 cup crystallized ginger,
  chopped
1/2 cup cooked rice
White pepper, to taste
2 tsp Better Than Bouillon™
  Chicken Base dissolved
  in 2 cups hot water or
  1 cup hot water and
  1 cup dry white wine
Lemon slices, cilantro leaves,
  or watercress sprigs (for
  garnish)

Place water and Better Than Bouillon™ Chicken Base in large stock pot. Heat to a boil, then reduce to a simmer. Add carrots, onion, potatoes, squash, parsley and bay leaf to stock. Add crystallized ginger and let mixture simmer slowly until all vegetables are fork tender (about 2 hours). Remove from heat and let mixture rest. Add rice, and when cool enough to handle, pour 2 cups at a time into food processor. Process until smooth and pour into clean stock pot. When soup is warmed, add white pepper, to taste. If soup is too thick, add Better Than Bouillon™ Chicken Broth until desired consistency is reached. Serve hot or chilled, garnished with lemon slices, cilantro leaves or watercress sprigs.

# TURKEY BREAST PICCATA WITH CAPERS

*Use Beef Base*
*Servings: 2*

Judith Tolchin

*1/2 lb turkey breast filet (also called turkey tenderloin)*
*Seasoned flour (with salt, pepper, paprika, and tarragon)*
*1–2 Tbs olive oil*
*1 Tsp Better Than Bouillon™ Beef Base dissolved in 1 cup boiling water*
*1 fat clove garlic, split in half*
*Juice from 1/2 lemon*
*6–7 fennel seeds*
*Fat pinch dried thyme or oregano*
*Salt and freshly ground pepper, to taste*
*1–2 Tbs drained capers*
*Optional garnishes: minced parsley, additional wedges or slices of lemon*

With a sharp knife, cut turkey breast on the bias into 6 or 8 thick slices (this is easiest to do when the turkey breast is partially frozen). Pat dry on paper towels. Pound slices between pieces of plastic wrap, 2–3 at a time, to about 1/8-inch thick. Heat oil in saute pan over medium-high heat. Dredge turkey in seasoned flour and saute on both sides until golden brown, 3–4 minutes per side. Remove and set aside.

Add Better Than Bouillon™ Beef Broth to hot pan, scraping up any browned flour or coagulated juices that remain. Add garlic clove pieces, lemon juice, fennel seeds, thyme or oregano, and salt and pepper to taste; bring mixture to a boil. Reduce heat and continue cooking until sauce is somewhat reduced & slightly thickened (3-5 minutes). Return turkey to the pan and add capers. Baste turkey with sauce and capers several times while heating through; remove garlic pieces, and taste carefully for seasoning.

Arrange turkey slices on plate so they overlap slightly. Spoon on sauce with capers. Sprinkle with parsley and tuck lemon wedges or slices around the meat. Serve with diced sauteed potatoes or boiled noodles, a green vegetable, salad, and crusty bread.

# GREEN CHILE AND CHEESE SOUP

**Suzanne Castillo**

*Use Chicken Base*
*Servings: 8*

3 Tbs cooking oil
1 cup chopped onions
3 garlic cloves, minced
2 cups tomatoes, chopped
8 Anaheim chilies (the kind used for chilies rel-lenos), roasted, peeled, deveined and diced
8 cups water
4 Tbs Better Than Bouillon™ Chicken Base
1/2 tsp basil
Salt and pepper, to taste
1 lb fresh panela Mexican cheese, cubed

In large pot sauté garlic, onions, tomatoes and chilies for about 3–5 minutes on medium-high heat (do not over cook). Add water, Better Than Bouillon™, and all spices. Cook, covered, 5 minutes on medium heat. Add cheese, cover and simmer on low heat for 1–2 minutes, until cheese is semi-melted, but not completely. Remove from heat and keep covered until ready to serve.

# STUFFED BELL PEPPERS

**Wayne Terry**

*Use Beef Base*
*Servings: 2*

2 red bell peppers, cored, halved, seeded
1/2 lb ground beef
1/2 cup bloody Mary mix
3/4 cup white rice, cooked
1 Tbs dry minced onion, reconstituted
1/2 Tbs seasoned salt
2 Tbs hot ketchup
1 tsp Better Than Bouillon™ Beef Base
1/4 tsp ground pepper

Place bell peppers in baking dish and fill one-quarter full of water. Microwave on high 4 minutes, or until peppers are semi-soft. Brown beef and drain. Combine with bloody Mary mix in microwave-safe container and microwave on high for 1 3/4 minutes. Stir well to combine. Combine beef with remaining ingredients. Fill bell peppers with meat mixture and bake at 350° for 20 minutes.

# PICKLE APPETIZER SANDWICHES

**Betty O. Lark**                    *Use Vegetable Base*
                                     *Yield: 12*

*1 cup fresh watercress or spinach, washed, patted dry, and minced*
*8 oz light cream cheese, softened*
*1 1/2 tsp Better Than Bouillon™ Vegetable Base*
*1 Tbs prepared horseradish*
*2 Tbs finely minced onion*
*1 tsp Tabasco sauce*
*12 sweet dill pickle strips, drained*

*12 slices white bread, crusts removed*

Combine all ingredients except pickles and bread. Spread thickly on bread and place one dill pickle strip on each. Roll bread and place sandwiches on a tray. Cover with dampened paper towel and refrigerate for 1-2 hours. Cut into 1-inch slices with a serrated knife when ready to serve.

# EASY ONION TART

**Patricia Schroedl**                *Use Vegetable Base*
                                     *Servings: 8*

*1 sheet frozen puff pastry (1/2 of a 17 1/4-oz box), thawed*
*2 Tbs butter or margarine*
*4 tsp Better Than Bouillon™ Vegetable Base*
*3 lbs onions, coarsely chopped*

Roll out pastry sheet into a 13-inch circle. Place pastry in an 11-inch tart pan with removable bottom. Trim edges and place in freezer.

Melt butter in large, heavy skillet. Stir in Better Than Bouillon™ Vegetable Base and blend well. Add onions and cook over medium-low heat until onions are browned and mushy, stirring occasionally.

Preheat oven to 400°. Fill frozen crust with onions and bake for 25 minutes, or until crust is golden.

# CAMILLA'S ORANGE-CILANTRO COUSCOUS SALAD

*Use Vegetable Base*
*Servings: 6*

**Camilla V. Saulsbury**

## C O U S C O U S

2 tsp Better Than Bouillon™
   Vegetable Base dissolved
   in 2 cups hot water
2 Tbs butter
1 1/2 cups couscous

## D R E S S I N G

3 Tbs freshly squeezed lime
   juice
1/3 cup freshly squeezed
   orange juice
1/3 cup olive oil
2 tsp honey
3/4 tsp ground cumin

1 1/2 cups chopped pecans,
   lightly toasted
1/2 cup golden raisins
1/2 cup chopped fresh
   cilantro
1 Tbs freshly grated orange
   zest
2 11-oz cans mandarin
   oranges, drained and
   coarsely chopped
Salt and pepper, to taste

In a medium saucepan, bring Better Than Bouillon™ Vegetable Broth and butter to a boil. Stir in couscous. Remove from heat, cover, and let stand for 5 minutes. Fluff gently with a fork.

In a small bowl, whisk together lime juice, orange juice, olive oil, honey, and cumin. Set aside. In a large bowl, combine couscous, pecans, raisins, cilantro, orange zest, lime zest, and mandarin oranges. Add dressing and toss gently. Season with salt and pepper to taste. Serve at room temperature.

# RICE ITALIANO
**Sharon Fridrick**

*Use Vegetable Base*
*Servings: 4*

2 cups water
2 tsp Better Than Bouillon™
    Vegetable Base
1 Tbs olive oil
1 bunch green onions,
    chopped (reserve tops)
1 clove garlic, minced
1 cup brown rice
1 medium zucchini, quartered
    lengthwise and thinly
    sliced
3 plum tomatoes, seeded and
    chopped
1 tsp dried basil or 1 Tbs
    chopped fresh basil
Parmesan cheese

In heavy saucepan, bring water to a boil. Stir in Better Than Bouillon™ Vegetable Base, olive oil, green onions (except tops), garlic, and rice. Cover, lower heat, and simmer for 35 minutes. Add zucchini, cover, and continue to cook for 5-10 minutes, or until rice is done. Stir in tomatoes and basil. Adjust seasonings to taste. Garnish with chopped green onion tops and sprinkle with parmesan cheese.

# CROCKPOT PINTOS
**Sandra Lee**

*Use Beef Base*
*Servings: 8*

1 16-oz package dried pinto
    beans
4 Tbs Better Than Bouillon™
    Beef Base
1 tsp garlic salt
1 tsp garlic powder
3 cloves garlic, minced
1/8 tsp cayenne pepper
1/4–1/2 cups chopped white
    onion
1/4 cup finely chopped
    carrot
1/4 cup chopped celery
1/8 tsp cumin
1/8 tsp thyme
1/4 cup prepared salsa

Place pinto beans in a large pot. Dissolve 2 Tbs Better Than Bouillon™ Beef Base in enough hot water to cover beans. Soak pinto beans in Better Than Bouillon™ Beef Broth all day (10–12 hours).

Drain pintos and place in crockpot with enough fresh water to cover. Add 1 Tbs Better Than Bouillon™ Beef Base. Cover and cook on high setting overnight.

In the morning, add 1 Tbs Better Than Bouillon™ Beef Base and all other ingredients. Reduce to low setting and cook for 2 more hours.

# BETTER THAN BAJA
# CORNISH GAME HENS

**Howard G. Barnes**

*Use Beef Base*
*Servings: 2–4*

*2 Cornish game hens, giblets*
*removed and minced,*
*skin removed from neck*
*3 cups orange juice*
*1 Tbs Better Than Bouillon™*
*Beef Base*
*1 cup tequila*
*2 Tbs Tabasco sauce*
*1 Tbs dill weed*
*1 clove pressed garlic*
*2 oz butter*
*2 thick slices onion, minced*
*3 Tbs honey*
*1/2 cup flour*
*Cold water*

In large mixing bowl, combine orange juice, Better Than Bouillon™ Beef Base, tequila, Tabasco sauce, and dill weed. Stir well so that dill weed is thoroughly wet. Add pressed garlic. Place Cornish game hens into mixture and marinate in refrigerator for 4 hours, turning hens every 30 minutes.

Preheat oven to 375°. Place hens on roasting rack, legs and wings up. Roast for one hour. Reserve marinade and baste after 15, 30 and 45 minutes. Add honey to a cup of the remaining marinade. At 50 minutes, baste hens with honey marinade. At the hour, remove hens from oven and allow them to stand for 10 minutes before serving. Garnish with slices of orange and minced parsley, and serve with white or wild rice with gravy.

While hens are roasting, brown minced onion in butter. As the onions begin to color, add minced giblets and neck. Simmer slowly over low heat. Turn giblets occasionally so they brown on all sides. When giblets are just browned, add remainder of marinade (without honey). Simmer 5 minutes. Thicken by adding flour and water gradually while stirring constantly. Remove neck and serve gravy in gravy boat.

# TANGY PAN-ROASTED TRI-TIP

Gary Yarbrough

*Use Beef Base*
*Servings: 6*

1 1/2–2 lbs beef tri-tip roast
or top sirloin steak, cut
1 1/2-inches thick,
excess fat removed,
scored 1/2-inch deep
on both sides
2 4-oz jars prepared horseradish
1 15-oz can whole berry
cranberry sauce
1 Tbs Better Than Bouillon™
Beef Base dissolved in
2 cups water
1 Tbs olive oil
Fresh parsley

Purée horseradish and cranberries in food processor or blender. Reserve half of the puréed mixture in refrigerator. Combine other half with Better Than Bouillon™ Beef Base.

Heat olive oil in cast iron skillet until almost smoking. Rub half of the horseradish/cranberry paste evenly over one side of the meat. Place meat in hot skillet, paste side down. Sear for 5 minutes, and while cooking, coat the top side of meat with the other half of the paste. Turn meat over, scraping bottom of pan. Sear the second side for 5 minutes.

Remove meat from skillet. When the mixture left in the pan is about to burn, add water to pan to deglaze. Bring liquid to a boil; lower heat to medium and return meat to pan. Meat should be half-covered with liquid; add water as necessary to keep the sauce from cooking away. Simmer at medium heat for 20 minutes on each side for a medium-well-done roast. Reduce cooking time by 5 minutes a side for medium rare. Sauce should be dark and thick. Add water, a tablespoon at a time, to thin, or simmer to thicken.

Slice meat across grain into 1/4-inch slices, and arrange on serving platter with horseradish/cranberry mixture in center. Garnish with fresh parsley.

# "MUNIFICENT" GAME HENS WITH BOURBON CURRANT SAUCE

*Use Chicken Base*

**Kent Phillips**

*Servings: 4–6*

*4 extra large rock Cornish game hens (the bigger the better)*
*1 1/2 cups butter, melted*
*1/2 cup bourbon (or any straight whisky)*
*1 jar black currant preserves*
*1 tsp Better Than Bouillon™ Chicken Base dissolved in 1/2 cup hot water*
*3/4 pkg fresh herb mixture for poultry, chopped*
*Salt and pepper, to taste*

### S T U F F I N G

*6 to 8 cups seasoned stuffing mix*
*1/2 cup white raisins*
*1/2 cup wild rice*
*1 cup butter, melted*
*1/4 pkg fresh herb mixture for poultry, chopped*
*1 tsp Better Than Bouillon™ Chicken Base dissolved in 1 cup hot water*
*2–4 Tbs bourbon/currant mixture (above)*

Mix one cup butter, bourbon, currant preserves, and Better Than Bouillon™ Chicken Broth. Melt mixture in microwave; add fresh herbs. Bring just to a boil, season to taste with salt and pepper, and set aside. Preheat oven to 425°.

Combine all stuffing ingredients except Better Than Bouillon™ Chicken Broth. Add Better Than Bouillon™ Chicken Broth until stuffing is as moist as desired. Stuff hens and place in baking dish. Pour 1/2 cup butter over hens and season to taste. Roast for 20 minutes. Reduce heat to 350° and continue cooking 30–45 minutes, basting often with bourbon/currant mixture.

# CORIANDER AND CUMIN PORK ROAST

**Richard Sejokora**

*Use Chicken Base*
*Servings: 8–10*

5–6 lb pork roast
2 cloves garlic, slivered
2 tsp Better Than Bouillon™
    Chicken Base
1 Tbs minced shallots
1 Tbs coriander seeds,
    crushed
1 tsp cumin
1/8 tsp fresh cracked pepper
    (or to taste)
1 Tbs flour
Olive oil, if needed
1 cup water

Stud roast with slivered garlic. Mix Better Than Bouillon™ Chicken Base, shallots, coriander, cumin, cracked pepper and flour into paste (a little olive oil may be used to thin if needed). Rub mixture on roast. Place roast on rack in shallow roasting pan and pour water in bottom of pan. Roast, uncovered, at 375°, basting occasionally until meat thermometer reads 160–165°. Let roast stand 20 minutes before slicing.

Skim fat off pan drippings. For an excellent gravy, add water if needed and/or thicken with a roux. Gravy is also excellent on turkey, goose or duck.

# ITALIAN WEDDING SOUP AND CROUTONS

Use Chicken, Vegetable, and Beef Bases
Servings: 4–6

## Carol J. Pilmer

### BROTH

1 fryer chicken, cut up
3 Tbs Better Than Bouillon™ Chicken Base
1 Tbs salt
1 bunch fresh parsley
1/2 tsp pepper
1 bunch fresh spinach or endive, chopped

### CROUTONS

7 eggs, well beaten
7 Tbs flour
1/2 cup shredded or grated romano cheese
1 tsp baking powder
1 tsp Better Than Bouillon™ Vegetable Base
1 heart of celery, finely chopped
1/2 cup fresh parsley, finely chopped

### MEATBALLS

1/2 lb ground round beef
1 egg
1/2 tsp salt
1/2 tsp Better Than Bouillon™ Beef Base
1/8 tsp pepper
1 Tbs chopped fresh parsley
1 clove garlic, chopped
2 Tbs grated romano cheese
2 Tbs dried bread crumbs

*Broth:* Cook all ingredients except spinach or endive in a crock pot with enough water to cover the chicken completely. Simmer all day. Remove chicken from bones when cool enough to handle. Strain broth. Cool in refrigerator overnight; skim the fat.

*Croutons:* Combine all ingredients thoroughly in mixing bowl; pour into jelly roll pan. Bake at 350° for 25 minutes. Cut into 1/2-inch squares while still warm. Drop into broth at serving time.

*Meatballs:* Mix all ingredients together; form tiny balls (about the size of the tip of your little finger). Microwave in glass plate covered with wax paper for 5 minutes on high power. Drain.

Heat broth, meatballs, and shredded chicken. Add fresh spinach or endive. Cook for 10–15 minutes.

# POLENTA WITH SAUTEED MUSHROOMS AND ONIONS

*Use Beef Base*
*Yield: 3 1/2 cups*

(Polenta a Bouillonesque)

**Sandra Fargo**

*4 tsp Better Than Bouillon™*
*Beef Base*
*4 Tbs margarine (divided in half)*
*1 6-oz pkg sliced white button mushrooms*
*1 medium-sized yellow Spanish onion (diced)*
*2 1/2 cups water*
*1/2 tsp salt (optional)*
*1 cup cold water*

Melt 2 tablespoons of margarine in a large skillet over medium heat. Sauté mushrooms and onions with 2 tablespoons of Better Than Bouillon™ Beef Base until mushrooms are soft and onions are transparent. Add 2 1/2 cups of water, 2–3 tablespoons Better Than Bouillon™ Beef Base and 1/2 teaspoon of salt (optional). Heat to boiling and add the remaining 2 tablespoons of margarine. Mix 1 1/4 cups of yellow cornmeal with 1 cup of cold water and combine with the boiling mixture, stirring constantly. Reduce heat to low and continue to stir until mixture thickens. Pour into a mold sprayed with non-stick cooking spray and refrigerate until set. Unmold, slice and heat slices in microwave.

# 'TIS THE SEASONED TO BE CHICKEN BREAD

**Mildred P. Hochheiser**

*Use Chicken Base*
*Yield: 1 loaf*

## BREAD

1 1/4 cups warm water
    (105–115°)
2 tsp honey
1 envelope active dry yeast
1 1/2 cups bread flour
3/4 cup whole wheat flour
2/3 cup regular or quick-
    cooking oats
3/4 tsp salt
Cornmeal

## FILLING

1 tsp Better Than Bouillon™
    Chicken Base
Grated rind of one lemon
2 tsp parsley flakes
1 tsp thyme
3/4 tsp savory
1/2 tsp powdered marjoram
1/2 tsp sage
1/4 tsp basil
2 1/2 tsp water

## GLAZE

1 egg white, beaten
1/2 tsp Better Than
    Bouillon™ Chicken Base

In a small bowl combine warm water, honey, and yeast. Let stand until foamy (about 5 minutes). Combine 1/2 cup bread flour, whole wheat flour, oats, and salt in the bowl of an electric mixer. Add yeast mixture and mix at medium speed for 2 minutes, then at low speed for 2 minutes. By hand, stir in enough of the remaining bread flour to form a dough. Turn the dough out onto a lightly floured surface and knead by hand about 10 minutes until the dough is smooth and elastic. Place the dough in a lightly oiled bowl and turn to coat evenly. Cover dough and let rise in a warm draft free area until doubled in size (about 1 hour).

Combine filling ingredients into a relatively smooth paste.

On a lightly floured surface, roll out the dough into a 10x15 inch rectangle. Spread filling evenly over the dough. Beginning with a short end roll up the dough. Pinch the ends and seam together to seal. Lightly coat a 9x5x3 inch loaf pan with margarine and dust with cornmeal. Place the dough, seam side down, in the prepared pan. Cover and let rise in a warm, draft-free area until almost doubled in size (about 45 minutes). Preheat oven to 375°.

Combine ingredients for the glaze; brush on the top of the dough. Bake 35 minutes, or until the crust is brown and sounds hollow when tapped. Cool in the pan on a wire rack 5 minutes. Remove from pan and continue to cool on the rack.

# SAUSAGE STEW

**Steve Massarella**

*Use Beef Base*
*Servings: 4*

4–6 *links fresh sweet or mild*
*Italian sausage, sliced to*
*one-inch pieces*
1 *large russet potato, peeled*
*and diced large*
2–3 *carrots, peeled and*
*sliced to one-inch pieces*
1 *large brown onion, peeled*
*and cut into slivers*
1 *large green bell pepper,*
*seeded and pitched, cut*
*into 1/4-inch strips*
2 *cloves garlic, peeled and*
*chopped*
1/2 *cup canned chopped*
*tomatoes or 1 tomato,*
*peeled, seeded, chopped*
3 *tsp Better than Bouillon™*
*Beef Base dissolved in*
*3 cups water*
1/2 *tsp Better Than*
*Bouillon™ Beef Base*
*Cooking wine*
6 *Tbs olive oil*
*Seasonings (such as basil,*
*sage, oregano, salt,*
*pepper)*
*Parmesan cheese*

In a large skillet over medium heat, quickly brown sausage and potatoes in 3 Tbs olive oil. Add carrots, Better Than Bouillon™ Beef Broth, and a splash of cooking wine. Bring to a boil, then cover and simmer over lowest heat 30–40 minutes, until sausage is fully cooked and tender.

Meanwhile, in a large pot, gently saute peppers, onions and garlic in 3 Tbs olive oil and 1/2 tsp of Better Than Bouillon™ Beef Base until soft, stirring in tomatoes about halfway through. Spoon in sausage, potatoes, and carrots including some broth from skillet. Stir and season to taste with basil, sage, oregano, salt, and/or pepper. Garnish with parmesan cheese.

# SPICED PORK CHOPS SMOTHERED IN APPLES AND ONIONS

*Use Chicken and Vegetable Bases*
*Servings: 4–5*

Jane Hasselbach Isomoto

4 lean center cut loin pork
    chops, 1/2-inch thick
2 onions, sliced
4 tart cooking apples, peeled,
    cored and sliced into
    1/4-inch rings
1 tsp Better Than Bouillon™
    Chicken Base dissolved
    in 2 cups boiling water
1 tsp Better Than Bouillon™
    Vegetable Base dissolved
    in 2 cups boiling water
1 clove garlic, minced
1 tsp ground ginger
1/4 tsp ground cinnamon
1/2 tsp ground coriander
1/8 tsp cayenne
1/2 tsp dry mustard
1 Tbs brown sugar
No-stick cooking spray

## RICE PILAF

1 Tbs margarine
1 carrot, grated
1/4 cup slivered almonds
Zest of 1 small orange
1/4 cup raisins
1 cup uncooked white rice
2 tsp Better Than Bouillon™
    Chicken Base dissolved
    in 2 cups boiling water

Preheat over to 350°. Spray a cast iron skillet (large enough to hold chops in a single layer) with no-stick cooking spray. Heat skillet over high heat, add chops, and brown well on both sides. Transfer chops to a covered oven-proof baking dish. Add Better Than Bouillon™ Chicken and Vegetable Broths to skillet with apples and onions. Simmer over low heat until apples and onion are slightly soft. Move apples and onions to the sides of the pan, creating a "well" of broth in the center. Add to the "well" of broth: garlic, ginger, cinnamon, coriander, cayenne, dry mustard and brown sugar. Simmer, uncovered, for 5 minutes. Stir all ingredients together. Pour over chops, smothering chops completely with apples and onions. Cover and bake for 45 minutes. Turn oven off and let chops rest in covered pan for 15 minutes before serving. Serve with Almond Raisin Pilaf.

*Rice Pilaf:* Melt margarine in heavy gauge saucepan. Add grated carrot and cook over low heat, stirring frequently for 5 minutes. Stir in almonds, orange zest and raisins. Cook over low heat 2 minutes, stirring frequently. Add rice and cook 2 minutes more, stirring frequently. Add Better Than Bouillon™ Chicken Broth and bring to a boil. Cover pan and cook over low heat 15–20 minutes. Fluff rice, cover again, and let rice rest in the pan for 5 minutes before serving.

# SIMPLY REGAL RED POTATOES
# FIT FOR A KING

*Use Any Base*
*Servings: 2–3*

**Mary Rose Merten**

*4 medium red potatoes
(about 1 lb), cleaned
and halved
1/2 cup water
1/2 tsp Better Than
Bouillon™ Base\*
1 bay leaf
1 large clove garlic*

*\* Any of the six Better Than
Bouillon™ Bases (Beef,
Chicken, Vegetable,
Lobster, Clam, or Chili)
may be used*

Combine water, Better Than Bouillon™ Base, bay leaf and garlic in a skillet and bring to a boil. Place potatoes, cut side down in boiling liquid. Cover, reduce heat to low, and cook 10 minutes. Turn potatoes, cover and cook 10 minutes more. Remove cover, turn potatoes again and cook slowly until liquid is absorbed and/or cooked down and potatoes are tender. Turn potatoes occasionally for even coating. Remove bay leaf and garlic.

# JAMAICAN JERK SHRIMP WITH ANGEL HAIR PASTA

*Use Chicken Base*
*Servings: 4*

**Mary Ann Lee**

8 oz angel hair pasta
6 tsp Better Than Bouillon™
    Chicken Base dissolved
    in 6 cups hot water

## JAMAICAN JERK SPICES

1 tsp onion powder
1 tsp ground thyme
1/4 tsp salt
1 tsp ground allspice
1/2 tsp crushed red pepper
1/4 tsp ground nutmeg
2 tsp ground cinnamon
2 tsp sugar
1 tsp cracked black pepper
1/4 tsp cayenne pepper
1 tsp dried chives

1 1/2 lbs large shrimp
    (16–20 count), cleaned
    and deveined
2 Tbs fresh key lime juice
1 rounded Tbs Better Than
    Bouillon™ Chicken Base
    dissolved in 1 1/2 cups
    hot water
3 Tbs peanut oil
1 Tbs grated fresh ginger
2 cloves fresh garlic, chopped
2 green onions, cut into
    1/2-inch slices on
    the diagonal
Grated parmesan cheese

Cook angel hair pasta in Better Than Bouillon™ Broth until tender, but still firm (about 4 minutes). Place in large serving bowl and keep warm.

In large bowl, blend together all Jamaican jerk spices. Add shrimp and toss well to coat entire shrimp. Set aside. In small bowl, combine lime juice and Better Than Bouillon™ Chicken Broth. Set aside.

Heat peanut oil in large skillet. Sauté ginger, garlic, and green onions for one minute. Add shrimp and sauté for about 3 minutes, until shrimp are pink and firm. Stir in Better Than Bouillon™ Chicken Broth mixture and heat for 30 seconds. Remove and pour entire contents over pasta. Stir once. Sprinkle grated cheese over top and serve immediately.

# NOTES

# NOTES

# APPETIZERS, SAUCES & GRAVIES

$W$hether you use appetizers as cocktail-hour finger foods or as scaled down versions of the first course, they are sure to set the tone for the rest of the occasion. Try simple appetizers to complement a fine wine, or more exotic ones to tantalize your guests and prepare them for new tastes to come. Remember, presentation is key. Pay attention to visual presentation: sometimes simplicity works best, other times creative garnishing is more appropriate.

$S$auces and gravies are also complementary features of a meal. Each of the following recipes includes serving suggestions. In general, gravies are used with meat and poultry and sauces are best with vegetables, pastas, or seafood. But do not limit yourself to these suggestions, part of the fun of cooking is experimenting with new flavor combinations.

# SAVORY STUFFED MUSHROOMS

**Thespi P. Mortimer**

*Use Beef Base*
*Yield: 12*

12 extra large, firm white
    mushroom caps, wiped
    clean
1/3 cup walnuts, finely
    chopped
1/4 cup unsalted butter, soft-
    ened
1 large shallot, finely minced
1 1/2–2 tsp Better Than
    Bouillon™ Beef Base
1/8 tsp seasoned pepper

Mix all stuffing ingredients
together until well blended. Fill
mushrooms with stuffing and place in
small greased baking dish. Bake at
400° for 15 minutes or until tops
begin to brown. Serve immediately or
at room temperature.

# HEARTY CHICKEN APPETIZERS

**Margie Hyman**

*Use Chicken Base*
*Yield: 7 dozen*

3 cups Bisquick-type baking
    mix
1 1/2 cups finely chopped
    cooked chicken or turkey
2 tsp Better Than Bouillon™
    Chicken Base
4 cups shredded mozzarella
    cheese
1/2 cup grated parmesan
    cheese
2 Tbs parsley flakes
2 tsp prepared spicy mustard
2/3 cups milk

Lightly grease large cookie sheet.
Thoroughly combine all ingredients.
Shape into one-inch balls and place
about 2 inches apart on baking
sheet. Bake at 350° 20–25 minutes
or until brown. Remove from pan
immediately. Serve warm.

# DILL DIP

Lisa L. Wood

*Use Vegetable Base*
*Yield: 1 1/2 cups*

3 Tbs fresh dill, chopped
3 Tbs fresh chives, chopped
1 Tbs fresh parsley, chopped
1 tsp Better Than Bouillon™
    Vegetable Base
1/2 cup sour cream
1 cup plain yogurt

Combine all ingredients and serve. Great with raw vegetables or chips.

# CHILI CHEESE STUFFED ROLLS

Inez Codeus

*Use Chili Base*
*Servings: 6*

1 1/2 lbs ground beef
1 can tomato soup
1/2 onion, chopped
2 Tbs Better Than Bouillon™
    Chili Base
1 can sliced olives
6 french rolls
6 oz cheddar cheese, grated

In a large skillet brown ground beef. Add Better Than Bouillon™ Chili Base and onions and sauté several minutes. Add tomato soup and olives; cook over medium heat for 10 minutes.

Slice off top of rolls and remove bread from the middle of each roll. Stuff roll with ground beef mixture and sprinkle with cheese. Replace tops of rolls and wrap in foil. Bake at 325° for 10 minutes or until cheese is melted (or microwave for one minute).

*Low-fat version:* Substitute ground turkey and non-fat cheese for ground beef and cheddar cheese.

# BUFFALO CHICKEN WINGS
**Chef Jorge Bruce**

*Use Chicken Base*
*Servings: 4–6*

*24 whole chicken wings
(about 4 lbs)*
*4 cups peanut oil or other
vegetable oil*
*1/4 cup unsalted butter*
*4 Tbs hot pepper sauce*
*1/2 tsp Better Than
Bouillon™ Chicken Base*
*1 Tbs white vinegar*
*Salt and freshly ground pep-
per, to taste*
*Celery sticks*

*1 Tbs habenero sauce
(optional)*

Rinse wings in cold water and pat dry.  Cut off small pointed tip of each wing and discard.  Cut the main wing bone and second wing bone at the joint to make 24 drumettes and 24 flat wing portions, salt & pepper to taste.  In a deep fryer, wok or heavy pot, heat oil to 375°.  Place about 1/4 of the wings in the oil and cook until golden-brown and crisp, about 10 minutes.  Remove from oil and drain well.  Cook the remaining chicken wings in the same manner.

Melt butter in a small saucepan and add hot pepper sauce, Better Than Bouillon™ Chicken Base, vinegar, and salt and pepper to taste.  Pour over chicken wings.  Serve with Blue Cheese Dressing (recipe page 34) or Tom's Zesty Barbecue Sauce (recipe page 32) as a dipping sauce for chicken wings and celery sticks.

*Extra-hot chicken wings:* Add 1 Tbs habenero sauce.

# SPINACH AND FETA CHEESE TURNOVERS

*Use Vegetable Base*
*Yield: 24*

### Patricia Hamill

### FILLING

*2 Tbs vegetable oil*
*2 onions, finely chopped*
*1 10-oz pkg frozen chopped spinach, thawed and well-drained*
*1/2 tsp Better Than Bouillon™ Vegetable Base*
*1 tsp dried dill weed*
*4 oz feta cheese, crumbled*
*1 egg, beaten*
*3 Tbs dairy sour cream*

*Filo pastry*
*1/2 cup butter, melted*

Heat oil in a sauce pan over low heat. Add onions and cook, stirring occasionally, until soft, but not browned. Stir spinach and Better Than Bouillon™ Vegetable Base into onions and cook 2 minutes. Stir in dill weed and cheese.

Remove from heat and cool. Mix in egg and sour cream. Cover and refrigerate until cold.

Cut pastry sheets crosswise into 2-inch strips. Work with one double strip of pastry at a time, keeping remaining pastry covered with damp paper towels or plastic wrap to prevent drying. Brush one strip with melted butter. Place a spoonful of filling in one corner and fold to form a triangle. Continue folding, keeping the shape, until whole strip is used; press to seal and brush top with melted butter. Repeat with remaining pastry. Place on baking sheets; bake 20 minutes at 400°. Serve warm.

# DOLMADES
**Patricia Motooka**

*Use Vegetable Base*
*Yield: 45*

1 8-oz jar grape leaves
2 Tbs olive oil
1 onion, finely chopped
1/4 tsp Better Than
    Bouillon™ Vegetable
    Base
2 cups cooked long-grain
    white rice
2 Tbs chopped fresh mint
1 cup toasted pine nuts
Salt and pepper, to taste
1 tsp Better Than Bouillon™
    Vegetable Base dissolved
    in 2 cups hot water
Fresh mint sprigs, if desired

## YOGURT SAUCE

1 cup plain yogurt
1/2 tsp Better Than
    Bouillon™ Vegetable
    Base
1 tsp tahini

Drain grape leaves and rinse well; then soak in cold water to cover to remove brine, separating leaves carefully. Drain and set aside.

Heat oil in a medium skillet. Add onion and cook, stirring until tender, but not browned. Remove from heat and stir in Better Than Bouillon™ Vegetable Base, rice, mint, 1/2 cup roasted pine nuts, and salt and pepper to taste. Place about 2 tsp filling on each leaf; roll up leaf, tucking in edges.

Arrange filled leaves close together in a large skillet. If necessary, make more than one layer, separating layers with left-over grape leaves. Pour in enough Better Than Bouillon™ Vegetable Broth to barely cover the leaves. Place a heat-proof plate directly on top of leaves; place a weight (such as canned goods) on top of plate. Cover and simmer 30 minutes. Remove from heat and cool. Cover and refrigerate until cold. Garnish with 1/2 cup toasted pine nuts and fresh mint sprigs, if desired. Serve with Yogurt Sauce.

*Yogurt Sauce:* Mix all ingredients thoroughly. Chill overnight to blend flavors.

# SPRING ROLLS
**Stephanie Hamill**

*Use Chicken Base*
*Yield: 8-10*

5 dried black mushrooms
1 tsp vegetable oil
2 eggs, lightly beaten

F I L L I N G

2 Tbs vegetable oil
1/2 lb boneless lean pork,
    cut into matchstick
    pieces
2 green onions, cut into 1-
    inch slivers
1 cup shredded cabbage or
    bok choy
1 cup bean sprouts
1/4 cup matchstick pieces
    bamboo shoots
1/2 tsp Better Than
    Bouillon™ Chicken Base
    dissolved in
    1/4 cup water
2 Tbs oyster sauce
2 tsp soy sauce
Dash white pepper
1 1/2 tsp cornstarch dis-
    solved in 1 Tbs water

8-10 spring roll wrappers
1 egg white, lightly beaten
Vegetable oil for deep-frying

Soak mushrooms in water to cover for 30 minutes; drain. Remove stems, discard; thinly slice caps. Set aside.

Heat one tsp oil in wide non-stick frying pan. Pour in eggs, tilting pan to evenly coat bottom. Cook just until eggs are set and feel dry on top. Remove from pan; let cool slightly. Cut into thin, one-inch long strips; set aside.

Heat wok; add 2 Tbs oil, swirling to coat sides. Add pork; stir-fry 2 minutes. Add mushrooms and filling ingredients except cornstarch solution; cook, tossing for 2 minutes. Remove from heat; toss in egg strips. Set aside to cool.

To fill each spring roll, mound about 2 heaping Tbs filling diagonally across one wrapper, keeping remaining wrappers covered to prevent drying. Fold bottom corner over filling to cover, then fold over right and left corners. Roll over once to enclose filling. Brush sides and top of triangle with egg white. Fold over to seal. Cover filled spring roll with a damp cloth while filling remaining rolls.

Heat oil for deep-frying to 360°. Fry spring rolls, 2-3 at a time, 2-3 minutes or until golden brown, turning occasionally. Serve hot, with Plum Sauce (recipe page 35) for dipping.

# SALSA
## Chef Jorge Bruce

*Use Chicken and Chili Bases*
*Yield: 1 1/2 cups*

4 Tbs light olive oil
4 small garlic cloves, minced
2 cups finely chopped peeled
    and seeded tomatoes
1/2 tsp salt
1/4 tsp oregano
1/4 tsp parsley
2 1/2 Tbs minced cilantro
1/4 tsp Better Than
    Bouillon™ Chicken Base
    dissolved in
    1/4 cup hot water
4 small jalapeno peppers,
    seeded and minced
1/4 tsp Better Than
    Bouillon™ Chili Base

In heavy skillet, sauté garlic in olive oil over low heat. Do not brown the garlic. Add remaining ingredients and simmer, uncovered, until sauce thickens, stirring occasionally. (For hotter sauce, add prepared habenero or pepper sauce.)

Serve warm with chips, eggs, tacos, etc.

# TOM'S ZESTY BARBECUE SAUCE
## Thomas Davison

*Use Beef Base*
*Yield: 4–5 cups*

3 cups ketchup
1/2 cup cider vinegar
1/4 cup Worcestershire
    sauce
1/4 cups light brown sugar
1 tsp Better Than Bouillon™
    Beef Base dissolved in
    1 cup hot water
1 tsp garlic powder
1 tsp salt or 1 tsp Better
    Than Bouillon™ Beef
    Base
Tabasco sauce (optional)

In 2-quart saucepan, combine all ingredients. Simmer, uncovered, over medium heat for approximately 15 minutes to thicken. Set aside to cool. Can be frozen for later use. Great on hamburgers, chicken and ribs. Add a splash of Tabasco sauce for spicier flavor.

Serve with hamburgers, hot dogs, chicken wings, smokey Joes, etc.

# ROYAL PEPPERCORN SAUCE

**Ellen Burr**

*Use Chicken Base*
*Servings: 6*

1 Tbs royal peppercorn mix-
    ture (red, black, green
    and white peppercorns)
1/2 cup cider vinegar
1 tsp Better Than Bouillon™
    Chicken Base
1 Tbs cornstarch
1 cup water

Simmer peppercorns and vinegar over low heat in a one-quart saucepan until liquid is reduced by one-half.

In small bowl, combine Better Than Bouillon™ Chicken Base with cornstarch and water. Add to peppercorn mixture and bring to a boil, stirring continuously. Lower heat and simmer for one minute or until mixture clears and thickens slightly. Serve hot over grilled chicken, pork, veal, fish, shrimp, game or burgers. Makes about one cup sauce.

To make sweet and sour sauce/glaze, stir in 1/4 cup crabapple, apple or guava jelly until melted. Makes enough sauce for 1 1/2–2 pounds meat.

*Variations:* Substitute Better Than Bouillon™ Beef Base when serving over steak or roast beef. Substitute Better Than Bouillon™ Vegetable Base when serving over grilled vegetables, tofu or vegetarian patties.

# BLUE CHEESE DRESSING

**Chef Jorge Bruce**

*Use Chicken Base*
*Yield: 1 1/2 cups*

*1/2 cup dairy sour cream*
*1/2 cup mayonnaise*
*1/2 tsp Better Than*
*    Bouillon™ Chicken Base*
*2 Tbs chopped green onion*
*2 garlic cloves, minced*
*1 Tbs white wine vinegar*
*1/4 lb blue cheese, crumbled*

Combine all ingredients in a medium-sized bowl. Refrigerate overnight for best blending of flavors.

# VINAIGRETTE

**Superior Touch**

*Use Chicken Base*
*Yield: 1/2 cup*

*2 tsp Better Than Bouillon™*
*    Chicken Base*
*1/4 tsp freshly ground*
*    pepper*
*2 Tbs wine vinegar*
*1/2 cup oil*

Measure Better Than Bouillon™ Chicken Base and pepper into a small bowl. Add vinegar and stir until the base dissolves. Stir in oil.

*Garlic vinaigrette:* In a mortar or small bowl, pound half of a garlic clove to a pureé with the Better Than Bouillon™ Chicken Base and pepper before adding the vinegar and oil.

*Mustard vinaigrette:* Mix about one tsp Dijon-style mustard or 1/4 tsp dry mustard with Better Than Bouillon™ Chicken Base and pepper before adding vinegar and oil.

# PLUM SAUCE
**Patricia Hamill**

*Use Vegetable Base*
*Yield: 1 1/2 cups*

1/2 cup crushed pineapple
1/3 cup mashed, seeded
    Chinese salted plums
1/4 cup pineapple juice
1/4 cup brown sugar
3 Tbs cider vinegar
3 Tbs apricot preserves
1 tsp Better Than Bouillon™
    Vegetable Base
2 cloves garlic, minced
1 tsp crushed red chili
    peppers

In a food processor, combine all ingredients except chili peppers. Process to a smooth paste. Transfer to a saucepan and add chili peppers. Bring sauce to a boil, reduce heat and simmer for 5 minutes, stirring constantly.

Use as dipping sauce for spring rolls (recipe page 31) or meatballs.

# HOT AS HELL HABENERO PEPPER SAUCE
**Chef Jorge Bruce**

*Use Vegetable Base*
*Yield: 1 cup*

1 cup cider vinegar
6 medium-sized habenero
    peppers
4 medium garlic cloves,
    halved lengthwise
14 black peppercorns
1/8 tsp salt
1/2 tsp Better Than
    Bouillon™ Vegetable
    Base

Place all ingredients in a glass jar or bottle with a non-reactive lid. Keep in a cool place or refrigerate.

Use as you would any hot sauce.

*Notes:* The longer the sauce is stored, the hotter it gets.

The habenero is the hottest chili in the world, so adjust the amount of chilies accordingly.

Try storing the sauce in a soy sauce jar with a plastic controlled inner cap for pouring.

# "BETTER THAN BOUILLON"
# WHITE SAUCE

**Superior Touch**

*Use Chicken Base*
*Yield: 2 cups*

2 Tbs butter
2 Tbs flour
2 1/2 cups milk
1 tsp Better Than Bouillon™
    Chicken Base
White pepper (optional)
Freshly grated nutmeg
    (optional)
Heavy cream (optional)

Melt butter in a heavy saucepan over low heat.  Stir in the flour to make a roux and cook gently, stirring, for 2–3 minutes.  Pour in all of the milk at once, whisking constantly to blend the mixture smoothly.  Add Better Than Bouillon™ Chicken Base, increase heat, and continue whisking while the sauce comes to a boil.

Reduce heat and simmer, uncovered, for about 40 minutes, stirring occasionally to prevent sauce from developing a top skin or sticking to the bottom of the pan.  Season, if desired, with white pepper and/or nutmeg.  Whisk again until the sauce is smooth.  Add a little heavy cream if you prefer a richer sauce.

# COCKTAIL SAUCE

**L. Caughman**

*Use Chili Base*
*Yield: I cup*

1/2 cup ketchup
1/4 cup tomato-base chili
    sauce
1/4 cup grapefruit juice
2 Tbs lemon juice
I Tbs thinly sliced green
    onion
I tsp prepared horseradish
I tsp Worcestershire sauce
2 drops liquid hot pepper
1/2 tsp Better Than
    Bouillon™ Chili Base

Combine all ingredients; mix until well blended. If made ahead, cover and refrigerate for up to 3 days. Serve with raw oysters, cold poached fish, or cold shellfish.

# ARTICHOKE SPAGHETTI SAUCE

**Superior Touch**

*Use Vegetable Base*
*Yield: 4 cups*

3 medium-sized artichokes,
    trimmed and thinly
    sliced
3 Tbs olive oil
I Tbs butter
I medium-sized onion, thinly
    sliced
1/4 tsp finely chopped garlic
2 cups canned Italian-style
    tomatoes
I bay leaf
1/2 tsp dried basil
2 tsp Better Than Bouillon™
    Vegetable Base
Pepper, to taste
Cooked pasta (recipe
    page vii)

Heat oil and butter and cook the artichokes, stirring constantly, for three minutes. Add the remaining ingredients and pepper to taste. Simmer, covered, stirring occasionally, until the artichokes are tender. Serve over cooked pasta.

# "BETTER THAN BOUILLON" TOMATO SAUCE

**Superior Touch**

*Use Any Base*
*Yield: 1 1/4 cups*

6–8 medium-sized very ripe
   tomatoes, peeled, seeded
   and diced
1/2 tsp Better Than
   Bouillon™ Base*
1 bay leaf
1 large sprig dried thyme
1 onion, sliced
1 clove garlic, crushed
2 Tbs butter
1 Tbs finely chopped parsley
1 Tbs basil leaves, torn into
   small pieces
Salt and freshly ground pepper, to taste
1–2 tsp sugar (optional)

\* Any of the six Better Than
   Bouillon™ Bases
   (Chicken, Beef,
   Vegetable, Clam,
   Lobster, or Chili) may be
   used

Place tomatoes in an enameled, stainless-steel or tinned copper saucepan with the Better Than Bouillon™ Base, bay leaf, thyme, onion, and garlic. Bring to a boil, and cook, uncovered, over fairly brisk heat for 10 minutes or until tomatoes have become a thick pulp. Remove the bay leaf and thyme.

Continue cooking, uncovered, over low heat until the sauce is reduced to appropriate consistency— about 10-15 minutes. Whisk in butter to richen the sauce. Whisk in parsley and basil; add salt and pepper to taste and sweeten with sugar if desired.

# BROWN GRAVY

**Ginna Boscarino**

*Use Beef Base*
*Yield: 3 1/2 cups*

6 Tbs butter
6 Tbs flour
1 rounded Tbs Better Than
   Bouillon™ Beef Base dissolved in
   3 1/2 cups water

Melt butter and stir in flour until smooth and light golden in color. Stir in water until blended. Blend Better Than Bouillon™ Beef Base into gravy. Simmer for 10 minutes.

# APPLE CIDER GRAVY

**Donna Gibson**

*Use Chicken and Beef Bases*
*Yield: 1 1/2–2 cups*

*3 Tbs unsalted butter*
*1/2 cup chopped Spanish onions*
*1/2 cup chopped celery*
*1 shallot, chopped*
*1 Granny Smith apple, chopped*
*2 cloves roasted garlic*
*1/4 cup all-purpose flour*
*3/4 tsp salt*
*1 dash cayenne pepper*
*1/2 tsp freshly ground black pepper*
*1/2 tsp thyme*
*1/2 cup apple cider*
*3 tsp Better Than Bouillon™ Chicken Base dissolved in 3 cups hot water*
*1 tsp Better Than Bouillon™ Beef Base*
*1/2 Tbs unsalted butter*

To roast garlic, cut one whole garlic head in half and place each half on a piece of foil. Drizzle each with olive oil, and sprinkle with salt and pepper. Cover each head of garlic in foil and bake at 350° for 45 minutes. When cool, squeeze to remove garlic cloves.

Melt butter in large skillet over medium-high heat. Add onions, celery, shallot, and apple. Sauté, stirring occasionally, until mixture is lightly brown and apples feel slightly soft. Reduce heat to medium and add garlic, flour, and dry seasonings. Cook until mixture is rich brown in color, whisking frequently and scraping bottom of pan. Add apple cider and cook one minute. Add Better Than Bouillon™ Chicken Broth and Better Than Bouillon™ Beef Base. Bring to a boil over high heat. Reduce heat and simmer 5 minutes, whisking occasionally. Remove gravy from heat and pour through a fine mesh strainer into a clean sauce pan. Push on solids in strainer to extrude all flavors. Whisk butter into strained gravy. Keep warm until ready to serve. Great served over Garlic Mashed Potatoes (recipe page 150).

# "BETTER THAN BOUILLON" CHICKEN GRAVY

**Chef Jorge Bruce**

*Use Chicken Base*
*Yield: 2 cups*

2 Tbs butter
2 Tbs flour
2 1/2 tsp Better Than
    Bouillon™ Chicken Base
    dissolved in
    2 1/2 cups hot water

Melt the butter in a heavy saucepan over low heat and stir in flour until roux is smooth. Cook, stirring constantly, for 2–3 minutes. When the roux stops foaming and is light golden in color, pour in the Better Than Bouillon™ Chicken Broth and whisk continuously until the mixture reaches a boil. Move the saucepan half off the heat, so that the liquid on one side of the pan maintains at a steady but very light boil. Cook for 30 minutes, skimming off the skin, until the sauce reaches the desired consistency.

# HOLIDAY TURKEY GRAVY

**Superior Touch**

*Use Chicken Base*
*Yield: 3 1/2 cups*

1/2 cup milk
1/4 cup flour
1 cup juices from roasting
    turkey
2 cups water
1 Tbs Better Than Bouillon™
    Chicken Base
1 Tbs browning sauce
Chopped giblets (optional)
Pepper, to taste

Mix milk and flour together in saucepan. Add remaining ingredients and heat to boiling.

# SOUPS & STEWS

$S$oup is satisfying as a first course or as an entire meal. Best of all, soups are easy to make using Better Than Bouillon™ as a base or broth. The following recipes feature traditional and contemporary soups which are certain to please the most discerning taste buds. Try a hot soup as a main meal on a cold winter night or a chilled soup as a light lunch during the heat of summer.

$L$ike soups, stews are easy to make and are wonderful as a meal on their own. Stews are usually a one-pot meal and can often be prepared ahead of time in a slow cooker or crock pot. Try pairing a stew with one of the Better Than Bouillon™ bread recipes for a delicious, hearty meal.

# CHICKEN TORTILLA SOUP
**Tulie Trejo**

*Use Chicken Base*
*Servings: 6–8*

## CHICKEN

1 3-lb chicken, cut up
8 cups water
3 Tbs Better Than Bouillon™
   Chicken Base
2 carrots
1 stalk celery
1 white onion, chopped
2 bay leaves
1/2 tsp thyme
1/4 tsp oregano
6 sprigs parsley
1/4 tsp ground black pepper

## SOUP

2 Tbs olive oil
1 green bell pepper, sliced
1 red bell pepper, sliced
2 white onions, sliced
8 cloves garlic, minced
4 Tbs chili powder
1 1/2 Tbs ground cumin
4 cups chopped, roasted
   tomatoes, peeled and
   seeded
1/2 cup firmly packed
   chopped cilantro
Salt and pepper, to taste
Fried corn tortilla strips
1 1/2 cups shredded
   Monterey Jack cheese
1/2 cup chopped green
   onions with tops

Place chicken in a Dutch oven and add remaining ingredients in first list. Bring to a boil. Reduce heat, cover, and simmer for 45–50 minutes. Allow chicken to cool in stock. Strain off stock and save for soup. Remove all skin and bones from chicken and shread the meat. Set aside.

Saute peppers and onions in oil for 5–7 minutes. Add garlic, chili powder, and cumin. Cook 3 minutes. Add chopped tomatoes and cook 10 minutes to reduce liquid. Add chicken stock, shredded chicken, and cilantro. Season to taste. Bring to a boil, reduce heat, and simmer 3 minutes. Skim to remove fat.

To serve, place tortilla strips in soup bowls, ladle in soup, and top with Jack cheese and green onions.

# MUSHROOM MAGIC
**Esther Saritzky**

*Use Chicken Base*
*Servings: 8*

## S O U P

3 Tbs plus one tsp Better
    Than Bouillon™ Chicken
    Base dissolved in
    2 1/2 qts hot water
1/3 cup dry sherry
2 small onions, diced
2 lbs fresh mushrooms, sliced
1 pkg dried porcini mush-
    rooms (optional)
Better Than Bouillon™
    Chicken Base, to taste
Pepper, to taste

## M A T Z O
## B A L L S

1-2 Tbs canola oil
2 large eggs
1/2 cup matzo meal
1 tsp Better Than Bouillon™
    Chicken Base dissolved
    in 5 tsp water

Combine Better Than Bouillon Chicken Base, water, sherry, and onion in a stock pot and simmer for 30 minutes. Add mushrooms and simmer 30 minutes more. (If porcini are used, soak them in hot water for 15 minutes and then add both porcini and liquid along with the fresh mushrooms.) Add Better Than Bouillon™ Chicken Base, to taste.

Serve alone or add the following small matzo balls to the soup.

*Matzo Balls:* Blend oil and eggs. Mix matzo meal with Better Than Bouillon™ Chicken Broth. Combine two mixtures and stir until smooth. Refrigerate one-half hour. Bring 1 1/2 qts water to boil in large stock pot. Wet hands with water and make balls about one-inch in diameter (handle lightly). Drop matzo balls into boiling water and boil for 35 minutes, covered. Drain water and drop matzo balls into mushroom soup. Simmer 5 minutes.

# ASPARAGUS SPRING SOUP

**Susan Matherly**

*Use Chicken Base*
*Servings: 8–10*

2 Tbs olive oil
1 medium onion, chopped
3 cloves garlic, minced
3 stalks celery, diced
3 lbs asparagus cut in 1/2-
 inch pieces, tips
 removed and reserved
 (discard white ends)
6 tsp Better Than Bouillon™
 Chicken Base dissolved
 in 6 cups hot water
Salt, to taste
1/2 tsp white pepper
1/2-1 cup half and half

Sauté onion and garlic in olive oil until soft. Add celery and chopped asparagus stalks. Sauté for 2 or 3 minutes. Add Better Than Bouillon™ Chicken Broth and bring to a boil. Reduce to simmer and cook 25 minutes. Process mixture in food processor or blender. Return to a clean pot. Steam or microwave asparagus tips. Add to soup. Add salt, pepper and half and half, to taste.

# MARLENE'S "JUMP-START" BREAKFAST SOUP

**Marlene Davis**

*Use Chicken or Beef Base*
*Servings: 2*

1 tsp Better Than Bouillon™
 Chicken or Beef Base
2 cups cold water
1 cup udon (Japanese) noodles
1 cup chop suey vegetables
1/2 cup cooked chicken,
 pork, shrimp, or beef,
 sliced or cubed
1/2-1 tsp cornstarch
 (optional)

Dissolve Better Than Bouillon™ Chicken or Beef Base in water while heating to a near-boil. If cornstarch is to be used to thicken soup, add it while water is still cold. Add noodles, vegetables and meat and simmer until heated through and larger vegetables are slightly wilted (about 5 minutes). Serve immediately.

# CHICKEN NOODLE YOGURT SOUP

**Syd Bigger**

*Use Chicken Base*
*Servings: 6*

1 Tbs oil
1 onion, chopped
8 tsp Better Than Bouillon™
   Chicken Base dissolved
   in 2 qts hot water
5 cloves garlic, minced
1 tsp thyme
1/4 cup low sodium soy
   sauce
5 springs fresh parsley,
   chopped fine
2 tsp basil
1 tsp mixed vegetable
   seasoning
3 carrots
 Salt or Better Than
   Bouillon™ Chicken Base,
   to taste
6 oz wide egg noodles
3 cups cubed cooked chicken
2 Tbs arrowroot
2 cups plain yogurt
7 green onions, chopped

Pour oil into stock pot. Add onion and cook for 5 minutes. Add Better Than Bouillon™ Chicken Broth, garlic, thyme, soy sauce, parsley, basil, vegetable seasoning, carrots, and salt or Better Than Bouillon™ Chicken Base, to taste. Cover and bring to boil. Reduce heat and simmer for 30 minutes. Stir in noodles and cook, uncovered, for 10 minutes. Add chicken and continue to simmer.

In separate bowl, stir arrowroot into yogurt and blend well. Add to soup, stirring as needed. Bring to a boil and allow soup to thicken. Garnish with chopped green onions.

# BETTER BELIEVE IT'S GOOD FOR YOU SOUP

**Audrey Greco**

*Use Chicken Base*
*Servings: 2*

4 tsp Better Than Bouillon™
   Chicken Base dissolved
   in1 qt hot water
1 cup spinach leaves,
   shredded
1 10 1/2-oz package tofu,
   cut into cubes
Coarsely ground black
   pepper, to taste

Heat Better Than Bouillon™ Chicken Broth to a boil. Add all ingredients and simmer for one minute. Top with coarsely ground black pepper and serve.

# CHILLED SUMMERTIME AVOCADO BISQUE

**Barbara Sudekum**

*Use Chicken or Vegetable Base*
*Servings: 6–8*

3 medium avocados, peeled
    and seeded
1 medium cucumber, peeled,
    seeded, and sliced
3 tsp Better Than Bouillon™
    Chicken (or Vegetable)
    Base dissolved in
    3 cups hot water
3/4 cup plain nonfat yogurt
2 Tbs lime juice
1 tsp salt
1 dash Tabasco sauce
Lime slices

In a blender, purée all ingredients except lime slices. Refrigerate for several hours. Serve thoroughly chilled, garnished with lime slices.

*Note:* For a thinner consistency, add another cup of Better Than Bouillon™ Chicken (or Vegetable) Broth.

# SOUTHWESTERN BEEF AND BARLEY SOUP

**Marjorie Ohrnstein**

*Use Beef Base*
*Servings: 4*

1 lb lean ground beef
1/2 cup chopped shallots
2 Tbs extra light olive oil
4 tsp Better Than Bouillon™
    Beef Base
3 cups water
2 1/2 cups prepared chunky
    salsa (hot, medium, or
    mild)
1/2 cup quick-cooking barley
1 15-oz can white Northern
    beans, drained and
    rinsed
1 15-oz can red kidney
    beans, drained and
    rinsed
4 Tbs sour cream
Cilantro sprigs

In a deep pot, heat oil and brown meat with shallots. Drain any liquid after browning. Add Better Than Bouillon™ Beef Base, water, salsa, and barley. Bring to a boil, reduce heat, and simmer for 25 minutes. Add beans and cook for 5 minutes longer. Ladle into soup bowls and garnish each bowl with a tablespoon of sour cream and a sprig of cilantro. Serve immediately.

# SPICY BLACK BEAN AND SAUSAGE SOUP

**Diane Kenduck**

*Use Chicken Base*
*Servings: 4–6*

*1 1/2 cups dried black
    beans, soaked in water
    overnight*
*3/4 lb hot turkey sausage,
    casings removed*
*1 large onion, chopped*
*1 stalk celery, chopped*
*5 tsp Better Than Bouillon™
    Chicken Base dissolved
    in 5 cups hot water*
*2 Tbs chopped fresh parsley*
*1/2 tsp dried basil, crushed*
*1 bay leaf*

Spray a large pot with non-stick cooking spray and heat over medium-high heat. Add sausage and sauté for about 5 minutes, or until meat is lightly browned, breaking up meat. Add garlic, onion, and celery, and sauté for 2–3 minutes, or until onions are translucent.

Add Better Than Bouillon™ Chicken Broth to pot, along with beans, parsley, basil, and bay leaf. Bring to a boil, reduce heat, and simmer, covered, for 1–1 1/4 hours, until beans are tender, but not mushy. Discard bay leaf. Purée a few ladlefuls of beans in food processor or blender. Stir puréed beans back into pot. Serve in bowls and garnish with plain yogurt and chopped green onion.

# CREAM OF MUSHROOM SOUP WITH CELERY AND SCALLIONS

*Use Chicken Base*

**Diane Lawson**

*Servings: 8*

5 Tbs butter
2 cloves garlic
12 scallions
2 cups chopped celery
4 tsp Better Than Bouillon™
    Chicken Base
2 cups water
2-3 cups mushrooms, minced
    or chopped (portabello
    mushrooms make this
    soup very special)
4 Tbs flour
8 oz sour cream
1 cup milk (skim milk, if pre-
    ferred)
1/2-1 tsp lemon pepper
Better Than Bouillon™
    Chicken Base, to taste
Fresh dill or parsley
    (for garnish)

Sauté garlic, scallions, and celery over low flame until yellow and soft. Cook covered for about 12 minutes, stirring frequently. Meanwhile, in separate pan, bring Better Than Bouillon™ Chicken Base and water to a boil.

When scallions and celery are cooked, gradually add flour while stirring. Add Better Than Bouillon™ Chicken Broth, continuing to stir. Simmer until mixture thickens. Remove from heat, cool slightly, and process in blender until smooth.

In a stock pot, add purée and mushrooms. While soup heats over low heat, slowly add milk. Add water, according to desired thickness and taste. Simmer an additional 10 minutes if using minced mushrooms, and 20 minutes if using chopped. Season to taste with additional Better Than Bouillon™ Chicken Base, if needed. Add sour cream just before serving and blend well. Garnish with a sprig of fresh dill or parsley. Soup can be stored in refrigerator for two days, or can be frozen.

# CHICKEN AND TOMATILLO SOUP

**Norm Jolicoeur**

*Use Chicken Base*
*Servings: 4–6*

*3 lbs chicken, quartered and rinsed*
*Salt and pepper, to taste*
*3 Tbs olive oil*
*1 medium onion, finely chopped*
*3 cloves garlic, minced*
*1 lb tomatillos, chopped*
*1 fresh jalapeno chile, seeded and minced (use 2 for a spicier flavor)*
*3 tsp Better Than Bouillon™ Chicken Base dissolved in 3 cups hot water*
*2 Tbs finely chopped cilantro*
*Cayenne pepper, to taste*

Pat chicken dry and sprinkle with salt and pepper. In a heavy saucepan, heat oil over moderate-high heat until it is hot, but not smoking. Brown chicken 5 minutes on each side, or until chicken is well browned. Transfer chicken to a bowl and pour off all but 2 Tbs of fat.

Sauté onion and garlic in remaining fat over moderately low heat until onion is softened. Return chicken to skillet and add tomatillos, chilies and Better Than Bouillon™ Chicken Broth. Cover and simmer for 15–20 minutes, or until chicken is cooked through. Remove from heat, transfer chicken to a clean bowl and let cool until it can be handled. Discard skin and bones and cut chicken into bite-sized pieces.

Process tomatillo mixture in a blender or food processor. Bring mixture to a simmer and stir in chicken and cilantro. Stir in cayenne, salt and pepper, to taste. Serve in bowls with a dollop of sour cream, grated sharp cheddar cheese and cilantro sprigs.

# COCONUT MILK SOUP

**Chelsea B. Machal**

*Use Chicken, Beef, or Vegetable Base*
*Servings: 4*

2 cups diced chicken
2 Tbs Better Than Bouillon™
    Chicken Base
3 shallots or 1 small onion,
    finely chopped
2 green onions
3 cups canned coconut milk
1/4–1/2 tsp crushed chile
    peppers
2 Tbs lemon juice
2 cloves garlic, chopped
1/4 tsp turmeric
Steamed white rice

Heat coconut milk and Better Than Bouillon™ Chicken Broth to boiling. Add chicken, onions, garlic, chile peppers, lemon juice, and turmeric. Simmer another 15 minutes. Scoop rice into bowls with large ice cream scoop. Ladle soup around rice and garnish with whole chile peppers and green onions.

*Variations:* Add finely sliced carrots, green beans or zucchini 5 minutes before soup is finished. For beef soup, substitute diced beef and Better Than Bouillon™ Beef base. For vegetarian soup, substitute 1 pound tofu and Better Than Bouillon™ Vegetable Base. (For better texture, freeze tofu in store package and defrost in warm water before cutting tofu into cubes.)

# SIMPLY DELICIOUS GARDEN VEGETABLE SOUP

**Sylvia Shellenbarger**

*Use Vegetable Base*
*Servings: 6–8*

7–8 cups water
4 oz spaghetti, broken into
    2-inch pieces (or any
    other pasta)
6–8 small zucchini, cut into
    bite-sized pieces (about
    3–4 cups)
2 Tbs Better Than Bouillon™
    Vegetable Base
6–8 medium tomatoes,
    peeled and cut into bite-
    sized pieces (including
    any juice)
Garlic salt, to taste
Pepper, to taste
Fresh herbs (cilantro, thyme,
    fennel, basil, etc.)

Boil water. Add pasta and simmer for 3 minutes. Add zucchini and simmer 4 more minutes. Add Better Than Bouillon™ Vegetable Base and reduce heat to low. Add tomatoes and cook until just heated through so that tomatoes are not overcooked. Season to taste with garlic salt and pepper. Garnish with fresh herbs such as cilantro, thyme, fennel, or basil.

# CREAMY POTATO BROCCOLI SOUP

**Joy King**

*Use Chicken Base*
*Servings: 10–12*

6 medium potatoes, peeled
    and diced
1 lb broccoli cole slaw,
    chopped slightly (or 1 lb
    coarsely shredded broc-
    coli stems)
2 stalks celery, finely diced
2 1/2 Tbs Better Than
    Bouillon™ Chicken Base
1/2 tsp pepper
1 Tbs onion powder
6 cups water
Salt and pepper, to taste
5 cups milk
3/4 cup flour

Place all ingredients except milk and flour in a large stock pot. Bring to a boil and simmer for 20–30 minutes. Add milk (nonfat if preferred) and flour (blended with a small amount of the milk). Stir until thickened.

# CAULIFLOWER SOUP

**Barbara Jenlink**

*Use Chicken Base*
*Servings: 4–6*

1 medium head cauliflower,
   chopped
1 small onion, chopped
4 tsp Better Than Bouillon™
   Chicken Base dissolved
   in 4 cups hot water
3/4 cup rice
Cream or milk
Salt and pepper, to taste
Nutmeg, to taste

Combine 2 cups Better Than Bouillon™ Chicken Broth with cauliflower and onion. Simmer until vegetables are tender. Purée mixture in blender or food processor. Bring remaining Better Than Bouillon™ Chicken Broth to boil and add rice. Lower heat, cover, and cook 30 minutes. Purée in blender or food processor.

Combine two mixtures and add cream or milk to preferred consistency. Season to taste with salt, pepper and nutmeg.

# COUNTRY CABBAGE SOUP

**Sharon Anderson**

*Use Vegetable Base*
*Servings: 6*

6 tsp Better Than Bouillon™
   Vegetable Base
6 cups water
1 head cabbage, quartered
   and sliced
4 large carrots, sliced
1 red onion, peeled and diced
2 stalks celery, diced
12 broccoli crowns
1 Tbs fresh tarragon
1 clove garlic, finely chopped
Pepper, to taste
1 Tbs seasoned salt
3/4 cup uncooked instant
   brown rice

In a stock pot, combine Better Than Bouillon™ Vegetable Base and water, and bring to a boil. Add cabbage, carrots, onion, celery, and broccoli crowns. Cover and simmer one hour, or until vegetables are tender. Do not overcook vegetables. Add tarragon, garlic, pepper, and seasoned salt. Simmer on low 20 minutes. Add rice, and simmer and additional 10 minutes.

# DILLED FISH AND POTATO SOUP

**Superior Touch**

*Use Clam Base*
*Servings: 4*

1 lb fresh or frozen fish fillets
2 ribs celery, chopped
1 small onion, chopped
2 Tbs butter
3 tsp Better Than Bouillon™ Clam Base dissolved in 3 cups hot water
2 medium potatoes, peeled and cubed
2 medium carrots, thinly sliced
1 bay leaf
1 tsp dried dill
Salt and pepper, to taste

Thaw fish, if frozen; rinse. Cut fish into one-inch pieces.

In a 3-qt saucepan cook celery and onion in hot butter over medium-high heat for 4–5 minutes or until tender, but not brown. Add Better Than Bouillon™ Clam Broth. Stir in potatoes, carrots, bay leaf, and dill weed. Bring to a boil. Reduce heat; simmer, covered, about 10 minutes or until vegetables are almost tender, stirring occasionally.

Add fish. Return to boiling. Reduce heat; simmer, covered, about 5 minutes or until fish flakes easily with a fork, stirring once. Season to taste with salt and pepper. Discard bay leaf before serving.

# FIESTA PARTY SOUP

**Derelys De Paolo**

*Use Chicken Base*
*Servings: 6–8*

1 1/2 lbs cubed pork (fat
   removed) or chicken
8 cups water
3 Tbs Better Than Bouillon™
   Chicken Base
3 Tbs ground cumin
3 cloves garlic, minced
1 16-oz container fresh salsa
   (mild or hot)

## GARNISHES

Hot white hominy
Shredded sharp cheddar
   cheese
Diced avocado
Sliced radishes
Fresh cilantro
Tortilla chips

Sauté pork in pan until it is no longer pink. Transfer meat into a stock pot and add all other ingredients, except garnishes. Cover and simmer for 20 minutes.

Serve very hot in large bowls. Pass garnishes for guests to add to their soup at the table.

# CURRIED AVOCADO SOUP

**Andrew Harrington**

*Use Vegetable Base*
*Servings: 4–6*

2 medium ripe avocados
2 tsp Better Than Bouillon™
   Vegetable Base dissolved
   in 2 cups hot water
1 1/4 tsp curry powder
1/2 tsp Better Than
   Bouillon™ Vegetable
   Base
1/2 tsp minced fresh ginger
2 Tbs lime juice
1 1/2–2 cups half and half

Blend all ingredients except half and half until smooth. Blend in half and half and chill. Serve chilled.

# CALIFORNIA CORIANDER-CARROT SOUP

**Martha Burr**

*Use Chicken or Vegetable Base*
*Servings: 6–8*

*1 tsp canola oil*
*2 cups chopped onions*
*1 Tbs grated fresh ginger*
*1 tsp ground turmeric*
*1 tsp ground coriander*
*1/4 tsp pure chili powder*
*1 lb carrots, trimmed and*
*   thinly sliced*
*1 qt water*
*2 Tbs Better Than Bouillon™*
*   Chicken or Vegetable*
*   Base*
*1/2 cup chopped cilantro*
*Salt or Better Than Bouillon™*
*   Chicken or Vegetable*
*   Base, to taste*

Heat oil in 2–3 qt saucepan over medium heat. Add onions, ginger, turmeric, coriander, and chili powder. Sauté for 5 minutes. Add carrots, one Tbs Better Than Bouillon™ Chicken or Vegetable Base, and enough water to cover. Stir and bring to a boil. Cover and simmer for 10 minutes, or until vegetables are tender. Purée mixture in a blender or food processor. Return to the same pan with remaining Better Than Bouillon™ Chicken or Vegetable Base and water. Simmer until hot. Season to taste with salt or Better Than Bouillon™ Chicken or Vegetable Base. Sprinkle each serving with a tablespoon of chopped cilantro. Serve either hot or chilled.

*Tip:* Stretch unused portions with cold buttermilk seasoned with additional Better Than Bouillon™ Chicken or Vegetable Base and spices.

# MEXICAN CHOWDER
**Christine Perrin**

*Use Chicken Base*
*Servings: 8*

1 large onion, chopped
3 cloves garlic, minced
3 oz butter
2 carrots, diced
1 red bell pepper, chopped
1 green bell pepper, chopped
1 large potato, peeled and
   chopped
3 Tbs Better Than Bouillon™
   Chicken Base dissolved
   in 8 cups hot water
6 oz Jack cheese, grated
6 oz cheddar cheese, grated
1 17-oz can creamed corn
1 cup canned diced ortega
   chilies
3/4 tsp chili powder

## GARNISHES

Chopped tomatoes
Sliced avocados
Chopped red onion
Cilantro
Flour tortilla strips

Sauté onions and garlic in butter until opaque. Add carrots and bell peppers. Continue to sauté slowly until tender. Boil potatoes in Better Than Bouillon™ Chicken Broth until tender. Remove potatoes and reserve broth.

Place 1/3 of the onion mixture, 1/3 of the cooked potatoes, and 1/3 of the grated cheeses in a food processor. Add some of the hot broth and purée. Transfer puréed mixture into a clean pot and process remainder of onion mixture, potatoes, and cheeses as above.

To the puréed mix, add creamed corn, chilies, and chili powder. Cook over low heat, stirring, until well blended and hot. Serve in large soup bowls with garnishes.

# BLACK BEAN SOUP
**Jim Williams**

*Use Chili Base*
*Servings: 4–6*

*12 oz dry black beans (or
canned black beans —
see variation below)*
*1 1/2 tsp salt*
*3 Tbs Better Than Bouillon™
Chili Base*
*2 Tbs vegetable oil*
*1 1/2 cups chopped onion*
*1 green bell pepper, diced*
*1 tsp oregano*
*1/4 cup dry sherry (optional)*
*1 14-oz can whole tomatoes,
chopped*
*2 tsp lemon or lime juice*
*Cooked bacon or ham,
chopped (optional)*
*2 tsp dried parsley*
*1 tsp garlic powder*

Place beans in a large bowl and add enough water to cover. Let sit overnight. After soaking, drain water and add to stock pot. Add enough water to cover beans. Stir in salt and Better Than Bouillon™ Chili Base and simmer, covered, until beans are tender (adding water, if necessary). In a skillet, heat vegetable oil and sauté onion, bell pepper, and oregano . Add to beans. Add sherry, tomatoes, lemon or lime juice, and cooked bacon or ham. Simmer for 15 minutes, covered.

*Variation:* Use 3–4 pounds precooked black beans instead of cooking dry beans.

# LINDA'S SPLIT PEA SOUP
**Linda Bernstein**

*Use Chicken Base*
*Servings: 4*

*4 tsp Better Than Bouillon™
Chicken Base*
*1 qt hot water*
*12 oz dried split green peas*
*1 small onion*
*6 carrots*
*2 stalks celery*
*1/2 tsp cumin*
*Salt, to taste*

Combine all ingredients in a stock pot and simmer for about one hour. Blend half of the onion and carrots and all of the celery in a food processor. Slice the remaining carrots into bite-sized pieces and add to soup. Thin soup with water to reach desired consistency.

59

# CURRIED CRAB AND MUSHROOM CHOWDER

**Superior Touch**

*Use Lobster Base*
*Servings: 4*

*1 cup sliced fresh mushrooms*
*1/4 cup chopped celery*
*1/4 cup chopped green onion*
*1 tsp Better Than Bouillon™*
*Lobster Base*
*2 Tbs butter*
*3 Tbs flour*
*1/2 tsp curry powder*
*3 cups milk*
*1 cup light cream*
*2 medium potatoes, cooked,*
*peeled, and cubed*
*1 6-oz can crabmeat,*
*drained, flaked, and*
*cartilage removed*
*1 Tbs snipped chives*

In a 3-qt saucepan, cook mushrooms, celery, green onion, and Better Than Bouillon™ Lobster Base in butter over medium-high heat for 4–5 minutes or until celery and onion or tender but not brown. Stir in flour and curry powder. Add milk and light cream all at once. Cook, stirring, over medium heat until mixture is thickened and bubbly.

Stir in potatoes and crabmeat. Heat through, stirring occasionally. To serve, ladle chowder into soup bowls and sprinkle with chives.

# SPLIT PEA AND LENTIL SOUP

**Barbara Fuller**

*Use Chicken Base*
*Servings: 4*

*1 Tbs Better Than Bouillon™*
*Chicken Base*
*1 onion, chopped*
*2 stalks celery with leaves,*
*chopped*
*1/2 cup dried split peas*
*1/2 cup dried lentils*
*4 tsp Better Than Bouillon™*
*Chicken Base dissolved*
*in 3 cups hot water*
*2 strips bacon, chopped*
*10–14 oz frozen mixed veg-*
*etables (optional)*
*Chopped cilantro or cucumbers*

Sauté chopped onion and celery in Better Than Bouillon™ Chicken Base until almost soft. Add Better Than Bouillon™ Chicken Broth and rinsed peas and lentils. Cook over low heat or in crockpot until done (approximately one hour on stove). Add bacon and frozen vegetables, if desired, just before serving. Top with chopped cilantro or cucumbers.

# JOSE'S TACO SOUP

**Joseph C. Tripcic**

*Use Beef Base*
*Servings: 6–8*

*1 3/4 cups ground beef*
*7 cups water*
*1 cup diced celery*
*2 cups diced potatoes*
*2 cups diced onions*
*1 7-oz can ortega green chile salsa*
*1 pkg taco seasonings*
*2 cups diced tomatoes*
*1 can condensed cheddar cheese soup*
*2 Tbs Better Than Bouillon™ Beef Base*
*2 avocados, thinly sliced*

In a small skillet, brown ground beef, stirring continuously and breaking into tiny pieces. Drain fat and set meat aside. In a large pot combine water, celery, potatoes, and onions. Bring to a boil and simmer for 20 minutes; add green chile salsa, taco seasonings, tomatoes, and ground beef. Continue to simmer for 15 minutes; add cheddar cheese soup and Better Than Bouillon™ Beef Base. Simmer for 5 minutes, stirring frequently. Serve with a generous garnish of thinly sliced avocados.

# TEN MINUTE VEGETABLE SOUP

**John Hosker**

*Use Vegetable Base*
*Servings: 4–6*

*4 cups water*
*4 1/2 tsp Better Than Bouillon™ Vegetable Base*
*1–2 cloves garlic, minced*
*2 Tbs dried soup greens (available in Kosher foods section)*
*1/2 cup alphabet-shaped pasta*
*1 cup cooked ham, cubed*
*1 cup frozen oriental vegetables (or other packaged frozen vegetables)*
*Roux, as desired*
*Salt and freshly ground pepper, to taste*

Combine water, Better Than Bouillon™ Vegetable Base, garlic, and soup greens in large stock pot and bring to a boil. Add pasta and ham pieces and stir. Lower heat and simmer 4–5 minutes. Add frozen vegetables, stir, and return to simmer. Remove from heat and thicken with roux, as desired. Season to taste with salt and freshly ground pepper. Serve hot with crusty bread.

## MUSHROOM BARLEY SOUP

**Fay Hermes**

*Use Chicken or Vegetable Base*
*Servings: 8–10*

*4 Tbs vermouth or white wine*
*2 medium onions, diced*
*2 cloves garlic, diced*
*2 stalks celery, diced*
*1 lb fresh mushrooms, sliced*
*1 cup barley*
*1/2 cup Bragg Liquid Amino or Tamari*
*1/2 tsp garlic powder*
*1/2 tsp salt*
*1 tsp chopped parsley*
*1 tsp dill weed*
*1/4 tsp black pepper*
*10 tsp Better Than Bouillon™ Chicken or Vegetable Base dissolved in 10 cups hot water*
*3 carrots, sliced*

In a large stock pot, heat vermouth over medium-high heat. Add onions, garlic, celery and mushrooms. Sauté 4 minutes. Add barley, seasonings, and Better Than Bouillon™ Chicken or Vegetable Stock. Reduce heat and simmer for 2–3 hours, adding carrots approximately 45 minutes before soup is finished. Add water to thin soup to desired consistency.

## CREAMLESS BROCCOLI SOUP

**Dorothy Ann Meier**

*Use Vegetable Base*
*Servings: 4–6*

*4 cups broccoli, chopped*
*1 large onion, chopped*
*1/4 cup rice*
*4 cups water*
*5 tsp Better Than Bouillon™ Vegetable Base*
*1 1-qt package powdered skim milk (do not reconstitute with water)*
*Salt and pepper, to taste*

Combine broccoli, onion, rice, and water in saucepan. Bring to a boil and simmer 25 minutes. Remove from heat. Add Better Than Bouillon™ Vegetable Base and dry milk. Purée in small amounts in blender or food processor. Reheat and season to taste.

*Variation:* Substitute broccoli with carrots and add one tsp ground cumin.

# CROCKPOT CHICKEN TORTILLA SOUP

**Connie Kocher**

*Use Beef and Chicken Bases*
*Servings: 6*

3 1/2 cups water
2 tsp Better Than Bouillon™ Beef Base
1 1/2 tsp Better Than Bouillon™ Chicken Base
1 16-oz can stewed tomatoes, chopped
2 cups chopped cooked chicken
1 4-oz can diced green chilies, undrained
1 2 1/4-oz can sliced olives
1 medium onion, chopped and sautéed
2 tsp chili powder
1 tsp cumin
1/2 tsp garlic salt
2 tsp Worcestershire sauce
6 corn tortillas, cut into 1/2-inch strips
Cilantro leaves

Boil water in stock pot and add Better Than Bouillon™ Beef and Chicken Bases. Pour broth into crockpot along with rest of ingredients except tortillas and cilantro. Cook on high for 4 hours. Place tortilla strips in bowls and ladle soup over them. Garnish with cilantro leaves and serve immediately.

# EGG DROP SOUP

**Superior Touch**

*Use Chicken Base*
*Servings: 4*

1 qt water
1 cup frozen peas
2 Tbs Better Than Bouillon™ Chicken Base
1 egg, beaten
2 Tbs chopped green onion (optional)

Combine water, peas, and Better Than Bouillon™ Chicken Base in a saucepan and heat to boiling. Drop egg into boiling soup; simmer uncovered for 5 minutes. Remove from heat and garnish with green onions, if desired.

63

# NEW ENGLAND CLAM CHOWDER

**Maureen Christensen**

*Use Chicken or Clam Base*
*Servings: 8–10*

1 cup finely chopped onion
1 cup finely chopped celery
1/2 cup finely chopped
    carrot
2 cups finely chopped raw
    potatoes
2 cans minced clams
2 tsp Better Than Bouillon™
    Chicken or Clam Base
3/4 cup butter or margarine
3/4 cup flour
1 qt half and half or milk
1 1/2 tsp salt
Pepper
2 Tbs vinegar

Place onion, celery, carrot and potatoes in a sauce pan. Cover with juice drained from clams and enough water to cover vegetables. Add Better Than Bouillon™ Chicken or Clam Base and simmer until vegetables are tender.

In a separate pan, melt butter. Stir in flour to make a paste. Stir in half and half or milk. Stir constantly so mixture does not scorch. When mixture begins to thicken, add vegetable mixture. Cook until chowder boils. Remove from heat and add salt, pepper and vinegar.

# DELICIOUS MUSHROOM SOUP

**Rita Pogan**

*Use Chicken Base*
*Servings: 6*

1/4 cup butter or margarine
1/2 cup sliced mushrooms
1/2 cup finely sliced white
    onion
1 Tbs lemon juice
3 Tbs flour
1/2 Tbs Better Than
    Bouillon™ Chicken Base
    dissolved in 4 cups water
Salt and pepper, to taste
2 cups half and half or milk
1/8 cup sherry
1 small bunch parsley,
    chopped
Paprika

Saute mushrooms and onions in butter. Stir in lemon juice and flour. Slowly add Better Than Bouillon™ Chicken Broth, stirring until smooth. Add salt and pepper, to taste and simmer 10 minutes.

Add half and half and sherry and heat just to serving temperature. Add most of parsley. Serve with garnish of parsley and paprika.

# HEARTY CHICKEN
# VEGETABLE SOUP

*Use Chicken, Beef or Vegetable Base*
*Servings: 4*

**Mary Ann Hardison**

1/2 stick margarine
1/2 cup flour
1 qt water
4 tsp Better Than Bouillon™
   Chicken Base
1 lb boneless, skinless chick-
   en breast, cut into bite-
   sized pieces and lightly
   browned on both sides
3/4 cup coarsely chopped
   onion
3/4 cup sliced carrots
3/4 cup sliced celery
3/4 cup frozen green beans
3/4 cup corn
1 16-oz can peeled, diced
   tomatoes with juice
1 tsp black pepper
1 Tbs freshly chopped
   parsley
1 tsp sugar
2 bay leaves
3/4 cup frozen peas
   (reserved for later)

Cook margarine and flour a bit, but do not allow to brown. Gradually stir in water. Add Better Than Bouillon™ Chicken Base, chicken, vegetables (except frozen peas) and seasonings. Bring to a gentle boil, reduce to simmer, and cook for 45 minutes to one hour. Taste and adjust seasonings. Add frozen peas 2–3 minutes before serving.

*Variations:* For Hearty Beef Vegetable Soup, substitute 3 tablespoons Better Than Bouillon™ Beef Base and one pound browned beef cubes. For Vegetarian Vegetable Soup, substitute Better Than Bouillon™ Vegetable Base and 1/2 cup brown rice and 1 cup lentils, canned beans or pasta (additional cooking time may be necessary).

# "BETTER THAN BEEF" ALBONDIGAS SOUP

**Beverley Kraemer**

*Use Beef Base*
*Servings: 6–8*

## M E A T B A L L S

*1/2 cup chopped onion*
*1 egg, beaten or 1/4 cup egg substitute*
*1/4 cup yellow cornmeal*
*2 oz ortega green chile peppers, chopped*
*1/4 tsp oregano, crushed*
*1/8 tsp black pepper*
*1/8 tsp cumin powder*
*1 medium potato, peeled and diced*
*1 lb lean ground turkey*
*1-2 tsp Better Than Bouillon™ Beef Base*
*1 carrot, finely chopped*
*1 cup cooked rice*
*1/2 bunch cilantro*

*1 Tbs prepared salsa or 1 1/2 teaspoons chili powder*
*1/4 tsp cumin powder*
*1 carrot, finely chopped*
*1/2 bunch cilantro*
*2 oz ortega green chile peppers, chopped*
*4 cups water*
*4 tsp Better Than Bouillon™ Beef Base*
*1 16-oz can Mexican-style tomatoes*
*1 8-oz can tomato sauce*
*1/3 cup chopped onion*
*1 clove minced garlic*
*1 Tbs sugar*
*1 tsp salt*
*1/4 tsp pepper*
*1/4 tsp dried oregano*

In a bowl, combine all ingredients for meatballs.  Roll into one-inch balls and set aside.

In a Dutch oven, combine all soup broth ingredients and bring to a boil. Add meatballs and return to a boil. Cover and reduce heat to simmer. Simmer 30 minutes.

# FRESH ROASTED CHICKEN VEGETABLE SOUP

**Vera Mularz**

*Use Chicken Base*
*Servings: 6–8*

## CHICKEN

1 whole roasted chicken or 6
   whole roasted chicken
   legs
12 teaspoons Better Than
   Bouillon™ Chicken Base
   dissolved in
12 cups hot water
1 onion
2 cloves
1 bay leaf
6 parsley sprigs

2 Tbs olive oil
3 cloves garlic, minced
2 onions, diced
2 carrots, diced
2 stalks celery, sliced
1 Tbs fresh marjoram
1 Tbs fresh thyme
1 Tbs Worcestershire sauce
1/4 cup parsley, finely
   minced
Salt, to taste
1/2 tsp pepper
2 cups spinach, finely
   shredded and chopped

Place chicken in stock pot. Add Better Than Bouillon™ Chicken Broth and seasonings. Bring to a boil. Immediately reduce heat to low simmer, and cook for 40 minutes. Remove chicken and seasonings, saving chicken for another meal. Strain stock, if necessary.

Heat oil in stock pot and add garlic, onion, carrot, and celery. Sauté until softened (about 8 minutes). Add stock and seasonings. Five minutes prior to serving, add spinach.

# BETTER THAN MAMA'S
# ONION SOUP

**Jane Ikemura**

*Use Beef and Chicken Bases*
*Servings: 6–8*

4 large onions, thinly sliced
2 Tbs butter or margarine,
    melted
8 cups water
8 tsp Better Than Bouillon™
    Beef Base
1 tsp Better Than Bouillon™
    Chicken Base
1/4 tsp black pepper
1/2 clove garlic, minced
2 Tbs soy sauce
1 tsp Beau Monde seasoning

Sourdough or French bread
    slices, toasted
Jack cheese, sliced

Place sliced onions in a large shallow roasting pan and drizzle evenly with melted butter. Bake at 450° for 20 minutes, stirring twice, until onions are soft and just beginning to brown.

Place water, Better Than Bouillon™ Beef and Chicken Bases, pepper, garlic, soy sauce, Beau Monde seasoning, and baked onions in large pot. Bring to a boil, cover, and simmer 2 hours. Ladle soup into oven-proof bowls and float a slice of toasted bread in each one. Top bread with sliced cheese and place under broiler until cheese is melted and begins to bubble.

# CHICKEN WITH RICE SOUP

**Superior Touch**

*Use Chicken Base*
*Servings: 4–6*

1 1/2 qts water
3/4 cup rice
3 Tbs Better Than Bouillon™
    Chicken Base
1 12-oz can or 1 1/2 cups
    cooked chicken, diced
1 8–10-oz pkg frozen dried
    peas and carrots
1 tsp dried parsley
Pepper, to taste

Combine water, rice, and Better Than Bouillon™ Chicken Base in a saucepan. Heat to boiling; cover and simmer 20 minutes (or until rice is tender). Add chicken, vegetables, parsley, and pepper, to taste. Return to boiling; cover and simmer 5 minutes.

68

# CURRIED CARROT ASPARAGUS SOUP

### Helen Schmidt

*Use Chicken Base*
*Servings: 8*

2 Tbs margarine
2 large carrots, peeled and
    cut
1 large onion, chopped
1 1/2 tsp curry powder
1/2 tsp lemon garlic spice
1 tsp Old Bay Seasoning
2 Tbs Better Than Bouillon™
    Chicken Base
3 cups water
1 lb fresh asparagus
1 Tbs lemon juice
1 cup plain yogurt

Yogurt
Diced red bell peppers
Chives, snipped

In large, covered pan, cook carrots and onion in margarine on low heat until tender (about 5 minutes). Stir in seasonings, Better Than Bouillon™ Chicken Base, and water. Add asparagus and simmer, covered, for 5 minutes, or until tender. Stir in lemon juice. Process mixture in food processor or blender until smooth.

Combine small amount of soup with the yogurt. Stir until blended, and gradually add remainder of hot soup. Stir until smooth. Cover and refrigerate overnight or several hours. Serve soup cold in clear glass mugs or small bowls. Top each with a small dollop of additional yogurt, finely chopped red pepper, and snipped chives.

# MINESTRONE GENOESE

**Thelma Bryan**

*Use Vegetable Base*
*Servings: 4-6*

1/4 cup olive oil
1/4 lb turkey ham, cut into strips
1 clove garlic, minced
1 Spanish onion, finely chopped
1/4 cup fresh parsley, minced
1/2 tsp dehydrated basil, crushed
1/2 tsp dehydrated thyme, crushed
1 large sweet potato, skin removed, diced
2 carrots, scraped and diced
2 celery stalks, chopped
2 large ripe tomatoes, peeled, seeded and chopped
1 10-oz pkg frozen Italian cut green beans
6 cups water
2 Tbs Better Than Bouillon™ Vegetable Base
1 cup elbow macaroni
1 1/2 cups cooked kidney beans, drained

## P E S T O

1 tsp Better Than Bouillon™ Vegetable Base
1 10-oz pkg frozen chopped spinach, well drained
1 tsp dehydrated basil, crushed
1/2 tsp crushed garlic
1/4 tsp black pepper
1/4 cup grated romano cheese
2 Tbs plus 2 tsp olive oil

In large saucepot, heat olive oil. Add turkey ham, garlic, onion, parsley, basil and thyme. Cook until onion is transparent. Add potatoes, carrots, celery, tomatoes, green beans, water and Better Than Bouillon™ Vegetable Base. Cover and simmer one hour. Bring to a boil and add macaroni. Cook until macaroni is tender, 8-10 minutes. Stir in kidney beans and simmer 2 minutes. Serve with pesto.

Pesto: Combine all ingredients in a food processor or blender. To serve, stir one Tbs of pesto sauce into each bowl of minestrone.

# WHITE BEAN STEW
**Marjorie Ohrnstein**

*Use Chicken Base*
*Servings: 6–8*

1 lb dried white beans
1 1/2 qts water
2 Tbs Better Than Bouillon™
    Chicken Base
1/2 cup chopped onion
3 cloves garlic, minced
1/2 cup chopped shallots
1/2 tsp seasoned salt
1/4 tsp lemon pepper
1 Tbs canola oil
1 4-oz can diced ortega
    chilies
2 tsp ground cumin
2 tsp oregano
2 tsp chopped cilantro
1/4 tsp cayenne pepper
1/4 tsp ground cloves
5 boneless, skinless chicken
    breasts, cooked and
    diced
1 cup grated cheddar cheese
1/4 cup chopped green
    onions

In a large stock pot, combine beans, water, Better Than Bouillon™ Chicken Base, onions, garlic, shallots, salt, and pepper. Bring to a boil, reduce heat, cover, and simmer until the beans are tender (about 1 1/4 hours). Add water, if needed.

Heat oil in skillet and sauté chilies for one minute. Add chilies and all remaining ingredients (except cheese and green onion) to the pot. Cook for 20 minutes longer. Remove from heat and ladle into bowls. Top with cheese and green

# SHERRIED STEW
**Heidi Krumes**

*Use Beef Base*
*Servings: 6*

2 lbs round steak, cut into
    1/8-inch strips
2 cups water
1 cup cooking sherry
1 Tbs Better Than Bouillon™
    Beef Base
1 envelope dried onion soup
    mix
Scallions, sliced

Preheat oven to 300°. Combine all ingredients (except scallions) in a 2-qt oven-proof casserole dish. Garnish with scallions. Bake, uncovered, for 3 hours. Serve over rice or egg noodles (recipe page vii).

# BETTER THAN BOUILLON ITALIAN STEW

**Colleen Myers**

*Use Beef Base*
*Servings: 8–10*

3 1/2 Tbs Better Than
    Bouillon™ Beef Base
8–10 cups water
1 lb Italian sweet sausage,
    cut into 1/2-inch slices
1 9-oz box tortellini pasta
1 9-oz box spinach tortellini
    pasta
1/2 lb cabbage, shredded
1 small green pepper, finely
    chopped
1 medium zucchini, thinly
    sliced
1 small red onion, finely
    chopped
1 medium tomato, chopped
1 Tbs chopped fresh basil
Salt, to taste
Pepper, to taste

Combine all ingredients and bring to a boil over medium-high heat. Reduce heat and simmer until vegetables are tender. Serve with grated fresh parmesan cheese, accompanied by French bread and a tossed green salad.

# SIMPLY CHICKEN STEW

**Stephanie Hamill**

*Use Chicken Base*
*Servings: 5–6*

1 2-lb chicken, cut up
1 Tbs olive oil
3 tsp Better Than Bouillon™
    Chicken Base dissolved
    in 3 cups hot water
1 large potato, cubed
1 medium turnip, cubed
2 medium carrots, cubed
1 medium green pepper, cut
    up into 1-inch pieces
1 medium stalk celery, cut up
1 small onion, chopped

Brown chicken in oil in a dutch oven. Add Better Than Bouillon™ Chicken Broth and heat to boiling. Reduce heat, cover, and simmer 2–2 1/2 hours.

Add vegetables and cook just until tender.

# LIGHTER AND HEALTHIER
# LOUISIANA CAJUN GUMBO
*Use Chicken and Vegetable Bases*

## San Diego Systems/Diagnostics Corporation
*Servings: 4*

2 lbs boneless, skinless
  chicken thighs
Olive oil
1 1/2 Tbs Better Than
  Bouillon™ Chicken Base
  and
1 1/2 Tbs Better Than
  Bouillon™ Vegetable
  Base dissolved in
  8 cups hot water
1 lb smoked sausage, kielbasa, or hot links,
  chopped into bite-sized
  pieces
1 lb medium shrimp,
  deveined and shelled
4 cloves garlic, finely minced
1 large Spanish onion,
  coarsely chopped
3 bell peppers (1 each green,
  red and yellow, or any
  combination), coarsely
  chopped
4 large stalks celery with
  leaves, coarsely chopped
1 16-oz pkg frozen okra
1 Tbs Worcestershire sauce,
  to taste
1 tsp Tabasco sauce, to taste
1 tsp freshly ground pepper,
  to taste
1 tsp seasoned salt, or to
  taste
Filé powder
Prepared long-grain rice
  (recipe page vii)

Cut chicken thighs into 1 1/2-inch chunks and brown lightly in olive oil. Add to stock pot with Better Than Bouillon™ Chicken and Vegetable Broth. Brown sausage lightly in same skillet and add to stock pot. Sauté garlic for 2 minutes. Add other vegetables and sauté for 5 more minutes, until slightly browned. Add to stock pot along with Worcestershire and Tabasco sauces, pepper, and seasoned salt. Simmer for approximately 2 hours. Add frozen okra and simmer an additional 2 hours. Remove from heat and add filé powder gradually, stirring constantly. Gumbo must not be allowed to boil again after addition of filé powder. Serve in large bowls over mounded rice.

# CHICKEN TAMAYO

## Gloria Chambers

*Use Chicken Base*
*Servings: 3–4*

3 whole chicken breasts,
    poached
1 onion
Whole cloves
1 tsp salt
6–8 peppercorns
5–6 stalks celery
Parsley sprigs
6 medium fresh tamales (not
    canned)
1 4-oz can green chilies,
    seeded
1 cup tomato sauce
1 cup ripe olives, pitted and
    sliced
1/2 cup seedless raisins
1/2 tsp chili powder
2 tsp Better Than Bouillon™
    Chicken Base dissolved
    in 1 cup boiling water
3 oz dry sherry
1 cup grated sharp cheddar
    cheese
1/2 cup grated parmesan
    cheese

Place poached chicken in deep kettle with tightly fitting lid. Insert several cloves in whole onion and add to kettle, along with salt, pepper corns, celery and parsley. Cover with boiling water, cover pot, and allow chicken to simmer until tender (approximately one hour, depending on size of chicken breasts. Cool mixture in broth. This step may be performed a day ahead.

Slice tamales crosswise (about 3/4-inch thick) and use to line a buttered, oven-safe casserole. Cover tamale slices with thick slices of boned chicken, strips of green chilies, and remaining tamale slices.

Combine tomato sauce, ripe olives, raisins, chili powder, Better Than Bouillon™ Chicken Broth and sherry. Pour mixture over tamales, sprinkle with grated cheddar cheese, then with grated parmesan cheese. Bake, uncovered, at 350° for one hour.

# COUNTRY FISH STEW
## Superior Touch

*Use Clam Base*
*Servings: 4*

*1 lb fresh or frozen fish fillets*
*1 15-oz can great northern*
*beans*
*1 small onion, chopped*
*1 rib celery, chopped*
*1 clove garlic, minced*
*1 Tbs butter*
*1 tsp Better Than Bouillon™*
*Clam Base dissolved in*
*1 cup hot water*
*1 small head cabbage,*
*coarsely chopped*
*1 Tbs snipped parsley*
*1 Tbs finely chopped*
*pimiento*
*1 tsp pepper*
*Parsley sprigs*

Thaw fish, if frozen; rinse and pat dry. Cut fish into one-inch pieces; set aside. Drain beans.

In a 3-qt saucepan, cook onion, celery, and garlic in hot butter over medium-high heat for 4–5 minutes or until tender but not brown. Add Better Than Bouillon™ Clam Broth. Stir in beans, cabbage, parsley, pimiento, and pepper and bring to a boil. Reduce heat; simmer, covered, about 20 minutes, stirring occasionally. Add fish. Return to boiling. Reduce heat and simmer, covered, about 5 minutes or until fish flakes easily with a fork, stirring once.

Garnish with parsley sprigs. Serve hot with warm, crusty bread.

# CHUCK WAGON STEW

**Mr. and Mrs. Spencer Johnson**

*Use Beef Base*
*Servings: 4*

*1 lb ground beef*
*2 medium potatoes, cut into*
*    1/2-inch cubes*
*1/4 cup dehydrated minced*
*    onion*
*3 Tbs Better Than Bouillon™*
*    Beef Base*
*1 16-oz can whole tomatoes*
*1 8-oz can cut green beans*

Sauté ground beef in 10-inch skillet until meat is light brown. Stir in potatoes, onion, and Better Than Bouillon™ Beef Base. Add liquid from tomatoes and beans to skillet. Heat to boiling, then reduce heat. Cover and simmer 15 minutes. Stir in tomatoes and beans. Break up tomatoes with a fork. Cover and simmer until potatoes are cooked (about 5 minutes).

# SAILOR'S STEW

**Phronda K. Smith**

*Use Beef Base*
*Servings: 6–8*

*2 1/2 lbs beef stew meat*
*3 Tbs red wine vinegar*
*2 tsp salt*
*1 tsp pepper*
*1 bay leaf, crushed*
*Pinch of dried thyme*
*3 slices bacon*
*Olive oil*
*1/2 bottle red wine*
*1 onion, chopped*
*3 cloves garlic, chopped*
*Peel of one orange, shredded*
*3 carrots, grated*
*3 tsp Better Than Bouillon™*
*    Beef Base*
*2 Tbs cornstarch dissolved in*
*    1/2 cup cold water*

Marinate beef in red wine vinegar, salt, pepper, bay leaf and thyme overnight. Fry bacon; cool and crumble. Sauté marinated beef in olive oil. Return bacon to pan. Add red wine, onion, garlic, orange peel and carrots. Simmer for 3 hours. Before serving, add Better Than Bouillon™ Beef Base and stir. Thicken with cornstarch mixture as needed. Serve over rice (recipe page vii).

# NOTES

# NOTES

# NOTES

# NOTES

# NOTES

# NOTES

# MEAT, POULTRY & SEAFOOD

$\mathcal{B}$etter Than Bouillon™ enhances the flavor of your meat, poultry, and seafood main dishes. That is because Better Than Bouillon™ is made from meat and selected spices which are balanced to harmonize with each particular flavor.

$\mathcal{W}$hile salt has been used over the centuries to flavor and preserve meat, our bodies actually need very little of it to function properly. In fact, high sodium levels in the body cause high blood pressure, which has been found to be one of the major causes of heart disease.

$\mathcal{W}$hen using Better Than Bouillon™, you may safely reduce or omit salt in the recipe without sacrificing flavor. While Better Than Bouillon™ is not sodium-free, it does have significantly less salt content than canned broth and bouillon cubes.

# BEEF BALI IN ALMOND SAUCE
**Lin Brennan**

*Use Beef Base*
*Servings: 6*

3 Tbs vegetable or peanut oil
1 1/2 lbs flank steak, cut
    into 1/2-inch strips
6 green onions, cut into
    2-inch diagonal slices
4 medium carrots, thinly
    sliced on the diagonal
2 tsp Better Than Bouillon™
    Beef Base dissolved in
2 cups hot water
1/4 cup sherry or apple juice
1 1/2 Tbs minced crystal-
    lized ginger
Salt, to taste
Pepper, to taste
1 1/2 Tbs cornstarch
1/4 cup cold water
1/2 cup chopped toasted
    almonds
Hot cooked rice (recipe
    page vii)
Parsley or cilantro sprigs, for
    garnish

Heat oil in a 12-inch skillet over medium heat. Brown steak strips on both sides. Add onion and carrot and stir-fry until vegetables are limp. Add Better Than Bouillon™ Beef Broth, sherry or apple juice, ginger, salt and pepper. Continue cooking for 10 minutes, stirring to blend well. Dissolve cornstarch in cold water and add to skillet, stirring until sauce thickens. Stir in almonds. Serve over hot rice. Garnish with parsley or cilantro.

# PORK AND VEGGIE RAMEN

**Marene Steinberg**

*Use Chicken Base*
*Servings: 4*

8 oz thin spaghetti
4 Tbs peanut oil
2 cloves garlic, crushed
1 Tbs minced fresh ginger
1/2 cup julienne carrots
1/2 lb ground pork
1/4 cup sliced onions
1/4 cup julienne black mush-
    rooms (soaked in water
    20 minutes)
2 cups diced cabbage
1 Tbs Chinese chili paste
2 Tbs sugar
1/8 tsp white pepper
2 tsp Better Than Bouillon™
    Chicken Base
2 cups water
1 Tbs cornstarch
2 Tbs cold water
1 pkg firm tofu, cut into
    1/2-inch cubes

Cook spaghetti in boiling water until soft. Drain and set aside. While spaghetti is cooking, pour peanut oil into a hot wok and sauté garlic and ginger until soft; do not brown. Add carrots and stir fry for one more minute. Add ground pork and stir fry for 2 minutes. Add onions, mushrooms, cabbage, and chili paste. Stir fry until pork is completely cooked. Add sugar, white pepper, and Better Than Bouillon™ Chicken Base, and mix well. Add 2 cups water and bring to a boil. Mix cornstarch with 2 Tbs cold water. Slowly add to pork mixture, stirring constantly. Remove from heat when sauce has thickened.

Fill 2 bowls with spaghetti and top with tofu. Spoon pork mixture over noodles and serve.

# BEEF SHORT RIBS

**Ginna Boscarino**

*Use Beef Base*
*Servings: 8*

### S H O R T   R I B S

5 lbs beef short ribs
Salt
Pepper
Rosemary
1 cup diced celery
1 cup diced carrots
1/2 cup red wine
Brown Gravy (see recipe
  below)

### G R A V Y

6 Tbs butter
6 Tbs flour
1 rounded Tbs Better Than
  Bouillon™ Beef Base
  dissolved in 3 1/2 cups
  water

Sprinkle ribs with salt, pepper and rosemary. Place in baking pan with diced celery and carrots. Bake uncovered at 350° for one hour. Add red wine and brown gravy. Cover with foil and bake 1 1/2 hours or until meat is tender when fork is inserted.

*Gravy:* Melt butter and stir in flour until smooth and light gold in color. Stir in water until blended. Blend Better Than Bouillon™ Beef Base into gravy. Simmer for 10 minutes.

# BRISKET OF BEEF MAGNIFIQUE

**Rita Hoskins**

*Use Beef Base*
*Servings: 6–8*

3-4 lbs beef brisket
1/2 tsp seasoned salt
1-2 garlic cloves, sliced
1 medium onion, chopped
Paprika, to taste
3 tsp Better Than Bouillon™
  Beef Base dissolved in
  3 cups hot water
1/2 cup sherry

Sprinkle seasoned salt in roasting pan and heat in oven. Place meat fat-side-down in pan and brown on all sides. Add garlic and onion and sprinkle paprika on top of brisket. Pour Better Than Bouillon™ Beef Broth over roast and add wine. Cover and bake at 325° for 2 1/2 hours.

# BRISKET DELIGHT SANDWICH

**Fred Murbarger**

*Use Beef Base*
*Servings: 10-12*

1 3-4 lb beef brisket
2 1/2 Tbs Better Than
    Bouillon™ Beef Base
    dissolved in 2 1/2 cups
    hot water
12 oz beer
2 cups V-8-style vegetable
    juice
1 medium onion, chopped
2 stalks celery, coarsely
    chopped
2 medium carrots, coarsely
    chopped
5-6 parsley sprigs
2-3 cloves garlic, chopped
3/4 cup parsley, chopped

Preheat oven to 350°. Spray roasting pan with non-stick cooking spray. Remove excess fat from beef brisket and score brisket cross grain in a diamond pattern. Place brisket in pan, fat side up. Add Better Than Bouillon™ Beef Broth, beer, and vegetable juice (use as much as needed to partially cover meat.)

Add remaining ingredients, except chopped parsley. Cover and bake for 40-50 minutes per pound, or until fork-tender. Let meat sit in pan juices for about 30 minutes, then remove meat from pan and drain grease. Strain juice through medium strainer and discard vegetables. Add remaining parsley to pan juices and keep warm.

Brown meat on barbecue grill or in broiler. Slice cross-grain. Dip meat slices in juice and serve on split French rolls. Serve juice on the side.

# "BETTER THAN" PORCUPINES

**Stella Wolf**

*Use Beef Base*
*Servings: 4–6*

*1 lb ground beef*
*2 Tbs finely chopped onion*
*1 egg, beaten*
*1 1/2 cup uncooked long*
*grain rice*
*1 tsp Better Than Bouillon™*
*Beef Base*
*1 Tbs canola oil*
*3 tsp Better Than Bouillon™*
*Beef Base dissolved in*
*2 1/4 cups hot water*

Combine ground beef, chopped onion, egg, rice, and Better Than Bouillon™ Beef Base. Shape mixture into one-inch meatballs.

Heat oil in skillet and brown meatballs on all sides. Pour Better Than Bouillon™ Beef Broth over meatballs. Cover and simmer for 30 minutes. Serve hot.

*Variation:* Make meatballs slightly smaller and serve with toothpicks as appetizers.

# PORK, SAUERKRAUT AND POTATO DINNER

**Nancy Jensen**

*Use Chicken Base*
*Servings: 8*

*1 tsp vegetable oil*
*1 medium yellow onion,*
*chopped*
*1 lb lean pork, cut into*
*1-inch cubes*
*2 lbs sauerkraut, drained, but*
*not rinsed*
*8-10 medium white potatoes,*
*peeled and cut into large*
*chunks*
*2 Tbs Better Than Bouillon™*
*Chicken Base dissolved*
*in 4 cups hot water*

In a heavy Dutch oven, lightly sauté onion and pork cubes in oil. Do not brown. Add sauerkraut, potatoes, and Better Than Bouillon™ Chicken Broth. Cover and bake at 325° for 1 1/2 hours. There will be a lot of liquid in the pan. Let cool and refrigerate for a day or two. Return to 325° oven and bake, covered, for another 1 1/2 hours, until liquid is reduced. Serve with rye bread, caraway seeds, and soft butter.

# HENRI JACOT'S PIE

Henri Jacot

*Use Beef Base*
*Servings: 10*

## PASTRY

5 cups flour
1 tsp baking powder
1/2 cup soft butter
2 eggs
1 tsp Better Than Bouillon™
   Beef Base dissolved in
   2/3 cup cold water

## FILLING

3 Tbs butter
4 medium onions, chopped
1/2 lb chorizo, skinned and
   sliced
1 lb pork, cut into small
   cubes
1/2 lb ham, cut into small
   cubes
1/2 lb veal, cut into small
   cubes
1 hot chile pepper, minced
Black ground pepper, to taste
1 egg yolk, slightly beaten
1 Tbs water
1 strand saffron
4 medium potatoes, chopped
2/3 tsp Better Than
   Bouillon™ Beef Base
   dissolved in 2/3 cup hot
   water

Place flour on table or chopping block. Make a hole in the center for the baking powder, butter, eggs and Better Than Bouillon™ Beef Broth. Blend well with hands until it makes a cohesive mass which does not stick to fingers. Let dough rest in a warm place in a bowl covered with a damp cloth while preparing filling.

In large skillet, heat butter and fry onion very slowly in covered pan. Before onion takes on color, add chorizo, pork, ham, veal, and chile pepper. Season with ground pepper. Cover and cook slowly for about 45 minutes, or until meat becomes tender. Add potatoes and sauté for one minute.

Preheat oven to 450°. Divide dough in half and roll out each portion on a lightly floured surface. Lift one piece of rolled dough carefully onto greased baking sheet. Reserve 4 tablespoons of liquid from meat mixture, and place rest on filling. Leave 1/2-inch around edge uncovered. Place second sheet of dough over filling and seal by pressing edges together. Brush top of pastry with egg yolk beaten with one Tbs cold water and crushed saffron. Cut a 1/2-inch air hole in middle of dough and bake for approximately 15 minutes. When crust has browned, remove from oven and pour 4 Tbs of reserved liquid through the air hole.

# SUPERIOR PORK CHOP DINNER

**Jean Burnham**

*Use Vegetable and Chicken Bases*
*Servings: 4*

5 Tbs Better Than Bouillon™
Vegetable Base dissolved
in 1 1/2 qts boiling
water
1 cup celery, cut into 1-inch
chunks
1 cup carrots, cut into 1-inch
chunks
8 1/2-inch thick pork chops
Mustard
Bisquick-style baking mix
Canola oil
Pepper
Ground sage
2 tsp Better Than Bouillon™
Chicken Base dissolved
in 2 cups hot water
1/2 can flat beer

Combine Better Than Bouillon™ Vegetable Broth, celery, and carrots in stock pot. Simmer until vegetables are almost tender. Drain, and reserve vegetables.

Rub pork chops with mustard and coat with baking mix. Sauté in oil on both sides until golden brown, but not cooked through. Place in baking pan and sprinkle with pepper and ground sage. Add Better Than Bouillon™ Chicken Broth and flat beer. Cover tightly with aluminum foil and bake at 350° for one hour. Serve over noodles (recipe page vii) with vegetables on the side.

# BABY BACK RIBS

**Joan Shepherd**

*Use Chicken or Beef Base*
*Servings: 4*

## P O R K   R I B S

2 lbs pork ribs
Better Than Bouillon™
Chicken Base

## B E E F   R I B S

2 lbs beef ribs
Better Than Bouillon™ Beef
Base

*Pork Ribs:* Smear ribs lightly with Better Than Bouillon™ Chicken Base. Sprinkle with garlic and/or onion powder and pepper, to taste. Bake at 350° for one hour.

*Beef Ribs:* Smear ribs lightly with Better Than Bouillon™ Beef Base and follow instructions for Pork Ribs above.

# VEAL BRATWURST MIT ZWIEBEL
# SAUCE UND ROSTI

*Use Beef Base*
*Servings: 4–6*

(Veal Bratwurst with Brown Onion Sauce)
Bernie Askew

## SAUCE

2 Tbs butter, margarine, or
   light oil
2 Tbs flour
1 tsp Better Than Bouillon™
   Beef Base dissolved in
   1 cup hot water
1/2 tsp ground black pepper
   (or to taste)
1 tsp finely crushed dried
   oregano, or to taste
1/2–1 cup dry cooking
   sherry
2 Tbs olive oil, butter, or
   margarine
1 large onion, quartered and
   thinly sliced
1 cup dry white wine

4–6 veal bratwurst

Make basic roux with butter and flour. Stir in Better Than Bouillon™ Beef Broth, making sure roux dissolves completely. Season with pepper and oregano. Add sherry and simmer for 5 minutes to thicken.

Meanwhile, sauté onions in olive oil until limp and translucent. Add white wine and simmer to reduce to about half. Combine brown sauce and onions. Simmer 5 minutes.

Cook bratwurst on barbecue grill (reduces fat) or sauté in skillet. Serve smothered with brown onion sauce along with the rosti, Swiss-style hash browns, and a green vegetable of choice. Rice makes a great substitute for the rosti.

# ENCHILADAS VERDE

**June Vasquez**

*Use Chicken Base*
*Servings: 6*

### S A U C E

1 tsp Better Than Bouillon™
   Chicken Base
1 cup water
1 7 oz can salsa verde
1/4 tsp garlic powder

6 corn tortillas
1 cup diced chicken
2 oz Jack cheese, shredded
1 Tbs cilantro, chopped
1 cup finely shredded lettuce
Sliced black olives (garnish)

*For the sauce:* Combine ingredients and simmer for 2 minutes to combine flavors.

Dip tortillas into heated sauce. Distribute chicken over tortillas and roll up. Place side-by-side in oven-proof 6x8 inch dish (spray with cooking spray for easy clean up). Pour remaining sauce over enchiladas and sprinkle with Jack cheese. Bake for 30 minutes at 350°. Garnish with cilantro, shredded lettuce and olives.

# EASY STIR-FRY

**Edward H. Mortimer**

*Use Chicken Base*
*Servings: 2–3*

1/2 medium cabbage, sliced
1 medium onion, coarsely
   chopped
4 mushrooms, thinly sliced
2–3 Tbs canola oil
4 slices sandwich ham, cut
   into strips

### S A U C E

2 Tbs light soy sauce
1 Tbs red garlic sauce
2 tsp Better Than Bouillon™
   Chicken Base

Stir-fry vegetables in oil for 1–2 minutes. Add ham and sauce mixture. Stir well over high flame for one minute. Remove from heat and continue to stir for 30 seconds longer. Serve with steamed short-grain rice (recipe page vii).

# PORK MEDALLIONS WITH PEPPERCORN SAUCE

Wayne A. Terry

*Use Chicken Base*
*Servings: 4*

*1/2 lb pork tenderloin*
*2 Tbs margarine*

## S A U C E

*2 shallots, minced*
*1/2 cup dry white wine*
*2 tsp Better Than Bouillon™*
*    Chicken Base dissolved*
*    in 1 cup hot water*
*1 Tbs green peppercorns,*
*    crushed*
*3/4 tsp dried thyme*
*2 tsp Dijon mustard*
*3 tsp flour*
*3 tsp margarine*
*3 tsp capers*

Cut pork tenderloin into 1/4-inch slices and flatten by hand. Heat 2 Tbs of the margarine and brown pork slices for 3 minutes each side. Transfer meat to a plate and keep warm.

Sauté shallots in pan juices. Add white wine and boil 5 minutes. Add Better Than Bouillon™ Chicken Broth, peppercorns and thyme to skillet and cook until liquid is reduced to 3/4 cup. Add mustard and stir until smooth.

Combine flour and margarine and blend well with the sauce to thicken. Add pork slices and heat to serving temperature. Top with capers.

# PEPPER STEAK

**Bea Krueger**

*Use Beef Base*
*Servings: 6–8*

*2 lbs steak, cut into cubes*
*1/2 onion*
*1 Tbs Better Than Bouillon™*
*    Beef Base dissolved in*
*    2 1/2 cups water*
*2 green bell peppers, cut into*
*    strips*
*1 can sliced mushrooms*
*Flour*

Place steak and onion in kettle Add Better Than Bouillon™ Beef Broth, cover, and simmer for one hour. Add green pepper and simmer until peppers are well cooked. Add mushrooms. Thicken juice with flour and serve over rice or noodles.

# GROUND BEEF TACOS

**Cary Chitwood**

*Use Beef Base*
*Servings: 8*

## F I L L I N G

*1 lb ground beef*
*3-4 medium radishes, diced*
*3-4 green onions, diced*
*1 clove fresh garlic, minced*
*    (or 1/2 teaspoon garlic*
*    powder)*
*1 medium jalapeño, minced*
*Salt and pepper, to taste*
*1 1/2 tsp Better Than*
*    Bouillon™ Beef Base*
*    dissolved in 1/4 cup hot*
*    water*

*1 pkg prepared taco shells*
*Grated longhorn or mild*
*    cheddar cheese*
*Shredded lettuce*
*Diced tomato*
*Hot sauce*

Brown ground beef, radishes, onion, garlic, jalapeño, salt and pepper in skillet over medium heat. Add Better Than Bouillon™ Beef Broth to browned ground beef mixture. Cover and simmer over low heat for 15 minutes. Remove from heat and drain meat in colander.

Add ground beef to prepared taco shells and garnish with cheese, lettuce, tomato and hot sauce.

# LIGHT BREAD CRUMB MEATLOAF

**John Humphreys**

*Use Beef Base*
*Servings: 4-6*

*1/2 tsp Better Than*
*    Bouillon™ Beef Base*
*    dissolved in 1/4 cup hot*
*    water*
*1 egg, beaten*
*1 1/2 cups soft bread*
*    crumbs*
*1/4 cup chopped onion*
*1/2 tsp ground sage*
*Pepper, to taste*
*1 lb lean ground beef*
*3 Tbs chili sauce*

Combine Better Than Bouillon™ Beef Broth with egg, bread crumbs, onion, sage, salt and pepper. Add ground beef and mix well. Shape into loaf pan or shallow baking dish. Bake at 350° for 45 minutes. Spread chili sauce over loaf and bake 10-15 minutes longer.

# EASY BEEF FILLING FOR TACOS AND BURRITOS

*Use Chili Base*
*Servings: 4*

Jim Willey

*1 lb lean ground beef*
*1 medium onion, diced*
*4 Tbs Better Than Bouillon™*
*Chili Base*

Brown ground beef, diced onion, and Better Than Bouillon™ Chili Base together in skillet. Remove from heat and serve in tacos or burritos. Garnish with cheese, lettuce, tomato and hot sauce.

# EASY FRENCH DIP SANDWICHES

Virginia Perez

*Use Beef Base*
*Servings: 10*

*1 3-lb rump roast*
*5 Tbs Better Than Bouillon™*
*Beef Base*
*1 Tbs oregano*
*1 Tbs crushed red chile*
*flakes*
*1 Tbs seasoned salt*
*5 cups water*
*1 onion, thinly sliced*
*4 doz French rolls*

Season roast with oregano, red chili flakes, and seasoned salt. Cover and bake at 350° for one hour, or until medium rare. Cool meat and reserve pan drippings.

Slice roast and place in juice. Add enough water to cover meat. Add Better Than Bouillon™ Beef Base and stir. Add onion and more oregano and red chile flakes, if desired. Cover and cook on stove until meat is tender. Serve on French rolls with juice in a small bowl for dipping.

# MEATBALL SANDWICH

**Carolyn McCoy**

*Use Beef Base*
*Servings: 8–10*

## SAUCE

1 medium onion, chopped
1/4 cup olive oil
3 cloves garlic, minced
1 28-oz can tomato sauce
1 28-oz can crushed tomato
3 Tbs fresh parsley, chopped
2 Tbs combined basil, thyme
    and tarragon
1 1/2 Tbs Better Than
    Bouillon™ Beef Base
1/2 tsp salt
1/4 tsp pepper

## MEATBALLS

1 1/2 lbs lean ground beef
1/2 lb hot Italian sausage (3
    links)
1 cup Italian seasoned
    bread crumbs
2 eggs
1 Tbs Better Than Bouillon™
    Beef Base
1 1/2 Tbs fresh parsley,
    chopped
1 medium onion, chopped
1/4 tsp garlic powder
Pinch salt
1/4 tsp pepper
1/4 cup olive oil

*Sauce:* Sauté onion slowly in olive oil until transparent. Add minced garlic and cook until tender. Add tomato sauce, crushed tomatoes, seasonings, and Better Than Bouillon™ Beef Base, salt and pepper. Simmer, uncovered, one hour. Remove from heat and reserve.

*Meatballs:* Combine all ingredients except oil. Shape into 1/2-inch balls. In large skillet, sauté meatballs in olive oil for about 20 minutes. Add meatballs to sauce and simmer, uncovered, for one hour.

Cut 8-10 sandwich buns (approximately 8 inches long) horizontally in a "V" shape. Place desired amount of meatballs and sauce inside buns, sprinkle with parmesan cheese, and cover with top of bun.

# EASY BEEF CURRY WITH RICE

**Jennie Morrissey**

*Use Beef or Vegetable Base*
*Servings: 4*

*1 large onion, chopped*
*2 cloves garlic, minced*
*3 Tbs oil*
*1 lb round steak, cut into*
*1-inch cubes*
*1 Tbs curry powder*
*2 tsp Better Than Bouillon™*
*Beef Base dissolved in*
*2 cups hot water*

R I C E

*1 cup white rice*
*2 cups water*
*2 tsp Better Than Bouillon™*
*Beef or Vegetable Base*

Sauté onion and garlic in oil until limp. Add beef cubes and curry powder and sauté until browned on all sides. Add Better Than Bouillon™ Beef Broth to skillet and simmer until meat is tender (about 1 1/2–2 hours). Thicken gravy with cornstarch, if necessary. Serve over rice.

*Rice:* mix ingredients and simmer until rice is tender and liquid has been absorbed (about 20 minutes).

# SWISS STEAK CANDLELIGHT SUPREME

**Rita Hoskins**

*Use Beef Base*
*Servings: 4–6*

*1 1/2 lbs round steak*

*Flour seasoned with*
*1/2 tsp seasoned salt and*
*1/2 tsp onion powder*

*Canola oil*
*2 carrots, sliced*
*1 small onion, sliced*
*2 stalks celery, sliced*
*2 tsp Better Than Bouillon™*
*Beef Base dissolved in*
*2 cups water*

Cut steak into serving-sized pieces. Dip in seasoned flour and brown on both sides in hot oil. Place vegetables in Dutch oven or roasting pan and cover with meat. Deglaze pan with Better Than Bouillon™ Beef Broth. Pour over meat and bake at 325° for one hour, or until meat is tender. Serve over rice (recipe page vii).

# TURKEY CURRY WITH SWEET POTATOES

**Donna Eaton**

*Use Beef Base*
*Servings: 6*

*2 1/2 lbs turkey, sliced 1/2-inch thick*
*1 Tbs plus 1 tsp Better Than Bouillon™ Beef Base*
*1/4 tsp cayenne pepper*
*4 Tbs vegetable oil*
*Juice of one lime*
*3 garlic cloves, crushed*
*2 medium yellow onions, finely chopped*
*1 large green bell pepper, seeds and stem removed, cubed*
*2 Tbs mild curry powder*
*1/2 tsp dehydrated thyme, crushed*
*2 tsp finely minced ginger root*
*1 tsp sugar*
*1 3/4 cups water*
*Flour*
*1 large ripe tomato, seeds removed and diced*
*2 medium sweet potatoes, boiled, skin removed and cubed*

Place turkey in shallow glass dish. In a small bowl, combine 2 tsp Better Than Bouillon™ Beef Base, cayenne pepper, 2 Tbs oil, lime juice, and 1/3 of crushed garlic. Pour over turkey and coat well, Cover and marinate for 30 minutes.

In a large heavy skillet, combine remaining oil and garlic, onions and bell pepper. Sauté 2 minutes. Add curry, thyme, ginger root, sugar, water and remaining Better Than Bouillon™ Beef Base. Simmer about 12 minutes. Transfer curry sauce to a bowl.

Dredge turkey in flour and add to skillet (add no additional fat). Cook over medium heat until turkey is browned. Pour curry sauce over turkey. Simmer 5 minutes. Add tomatoes and sweet potatoes. Simmer an additional 2 minutes. Serve hot.

# CHRIS' COMPANY CHICKEN

**Chris Williams**

*Use Chicken Base*
*Servings: 8–10*

*10 chicken breasts, boned*
*    and skinned*
*2 eggs*
*1/3 cup milk*
*36 crackers, crushed*
*3/4-1 cup olive or vegetable*
*    oil*

### S A U C E

*1-1/2 cups warm water*
*2 cloves garlic, finely*
*    chopped*
*1/2 tsp pepper*
*2 tsp Better Than Bouillon™*
*    Chicken Base*
*1 Tbs lemon juice*
*1 Tbs white wine*

Rinse chicken in water, pat dry, and lay between two sheets of wax paper or cellophane wrap. Pound chicken with bottom of glass or rolling pin until nearly double in size.

Mix eggs and milk with fork in large bowl. Place pounded chicken breasts into mixture. Dredge both sides of chicken breasts with cracker crumbs.

Heat oil in skillet on medium heat. Brown both sides of chicken breasts in oil until light golden brown. Place chicken on cookie sheet.

Mix water, garlic, pepper, Better Than Bouillon™ Chicken Base, lemon juice, and wine in bowl. Pour over chicken. Cover with foil and bake in oven at 325° for 1 1/2 hours (bake uncovered for last 10 minutes). Serve with rice or pasta (recipe page vii).

*Note:* Works great from freezer to oven if unexpected guests arrive. Allow 2 hours for baking.

# TURKEY BARBY-Q-HAMBURGERS
**John Laury**

*Use Beef Base*
*Servings: 8*

1 5 1/2-oz (small can)
  tomato juice
2 Tbs Better Than Bouillon™
  Beef Base
1 Tbs fresh lemon juice
3 Tbs dehydrated chopped
  onion
2 Tbs dehydrated green
  pepper flakes
1/2 tsp freshly ground
  pepper
2 lbs lean ground round
  steak (or ground turkey
  or chicken)
2 eggs, lightly beaten
1/2 cup plain bread crumbs
Dijon-style mustard

In a small saucepan, heat the tomato juice, Better Than Bouillon™ Beef Base, lemon juice, onion, green pepper flakes, and ground pepper. Bring just to a boil. Remove from heat and stir until well dissolved

In a 3-quart mixing bowl, combine meat and lightly beaten eggs. Pour liquid mixture over meat and add bread crumbs. Work mixture together with hands and form 8 equal patties. Stack patties in a covered container, layering with waxed paper. Chill, covered, for one hour or overnight.

Barbecue (or broil) for 5 minutes on each side over medium heat, or until juices run nearly clear when pierced with a fork. Serve hot, brushed lightly with Dijon-style mustard.

# BETTER THAN BAKED CHICKEN

**Nita Folsom**

*Use Chicken Base*
*Servings: 4*

*1/2 cup flour*
*1 1/2 tsp salt*
*1 tsp paprika*
*1/4 tsp pepper*
*1 3–4 lb chicken, cut up and*
*    skin removed*
*Water*
*3 Tbs butter or margarine*
*2 tsp Better Than Bouillon™*
*    Chicken Base dissolved*
*    in 2 cups hot water*
*2/3 cups nonfat dry milk*
*    powder*

Preheat oven to 350°. Mix flour, salt, paprika, and pepper on a piece of wax paper or flat bottomed bowl. Spray a 9x13 inch pan with vegetable spray. Dip chicken pieces in water and coat with the dry mixture. Place in pan and dot with butter. Bake in oven for 30 minutes.

Add dry milk to Better Than Bouillon™ Chicken Broth. Remove chicken from oven after 30 minutes and pour milk-bouillon mixture around chicken. Continue baking for another hour, or until fully cooked. Serve with rice (recipe page vii).

# ARROZ CON POLLO

**Jim Williams**

*Use Chili Base*
*Servings: 4–6*

*1 cooked chicken, cut into*
*    pieces*
*2 Tbs butter or margarine*
*1 1/2 cups uncooked rice*
*1 medium onion, diced*
*1/2 tsp garlic powder*
*3 cups water*
*1 cup frozen peas*
*1 8-oz can tomato sauce*
*1 Tbs Better Than Bouillon™*
*    Chili Base*
*1 small can (4 1/4 oz) sliced*
*    olives*

Melt butter in saucepan and add rice, onion, garlic, water, peas, and Better Than Bouillon™ Chili Base. Bring to a boil and simmer for 20–25 minutes, or until rice is tender. Remove from heat. Stir in cooked chicken and olives. May be served immediately.

# CHICKEN JERUSALEM

**Rita Hoskins**

*Use Chicken Base*
*Servings: 4–6*

4–6 boneless, skinless
   chicken breasts
Flour
Salt
Pepper
1 egg beaten with
   2 Tbs milk or water
1 cup cornflake crumbs
Vegetable oil
4 Tbs flour
1 cup water
1/2 cup sherry
2 tsp Better Than Bouillon™
   Chicken Base
1 large can artichoke hearts
   or 1 pkg frozen arti-
   chokes, cooked
12 whole mushrooms or 1
   can mushrooms, drained

Rinse chicken and pat dry.
Season flour with salt and pepper.
Dredge chicken in seasoned flour,
then egg, and then cornflake crumbs.
Heat oil in skillet and brown chicken
on both sides. Remove from pan and
place in baking dish coated with non-
stick cooking spray. Add 4 Tbs flour
to pan drippings and stir. Add liquid
ingredients and stir. Mix in Better
Than Bouillon™ Chicken Base until
thickened. Pour mixture over chicken
and add fresh mushrooms.

Cover pan and bake at 325° for
1/2 hour. Uncover and add artichoke
hearts and canned mushrooms (if
fresh mushrooms are not used). Bake
uncovered 15 minutes longer.

# AFTER A HARD DAY CHICKEN

**Mae Canaga**

*Use Chicken Base*
*Servings: 4–6*

1 pkg skinless boneless
   chicken breasts cut into
   1/2-inch slices
2 Tbs olive or vegetable oil
1/4 cup balsamic vinegar
1 tsp Better Than Bouillon™
   Chicken Base dissolved
   in 1/4 cup hot water
1 Tbs flour

Brown chicken in oil until meat is
no longer pink. Remove chicken to
serving dish. Deglaze pan with vinegar. Add Better Than Bouillon™
Chicken Broth and bring to a boil.
Whisk in flour and cook to thicken
slightly. Drizzle hot mixture over
chicken and serve.

*Variation:* Add mushrooms,
capers, olives, or anchovies.

# GREEK CHICKEN

**Bill Kehayias**

*Use Chicken Base*
*Servings: 2*

*2 large skinless chicken
   breasts, bone attached
Pepper, to taste
Garlic powder, to taste
Crushed Greek oregano
   leaves
Juice of one lemon
Paprika, to taste
1 tsp Better Than Bouillon™
   Chicken Base dissolved
   in 1 cup hot water
Non-stick cooking spray*

Spray skillet with non-stick cooking spray. Heat skillet and add chicken breasts, meat side down. Brown surfaces on high heat for 3-5 minutes.

Meanwhile, season cavity of chicken breasts with pepper, garlic powder, and oregano. Reduce heat to medium-low, turn chicken meat-side up, and pierce meat with fork. Add liberal amount of lemon juice, pepper, oregano, and paprika. Add Better Than Bouillon™ Chicken Broth and additional lemon juice, to taste. Cover and simmer on low heat for 18-20 minutes. Remove from heat, turn chicken over, and let sit for 5 minutes to absorb flavors. Separate liquids and use as a dip for each portion of chicken.

# LOWFAT YOGURT CHICKEN

**Joan McKnight**

*Use Chicken Base*
*Servings: 3*

*8 chicken thighs, skin and fat
   removed
1 Tbs olive oil
1 cup chopped onion
3 tsp paprika
2 tsp Better Than Bouillon™
   Chicken Base dissolved
   in 2 cups hot water
2 Tbs cornstarch
2/3 cup nonfat plain yogurt*

Sauté onion in oil until translucent. Add paprika, Better Than Bouillon™ Chicken Broth, and chicken; simmer one hour, turning once.

Mix cornstarch and yogurt until smooth. Stir in 2/3 cup of hot broth to warm, then add yogurt mixture back into chicken. Cook five minutes to thicken. Serve over rice or pasta (recipe page vii).

# TURKEY MEATBALLS AND GRAVY

**Chris Williams**

*Use Chicken Base*
*Servings: 4–6*

## MEATBALLS

1 lb ground turkey
1 egg
1/2 cup cracker crumbs or
   dry bread crumbs
1/8 cup milk
1/8 cup Better Than
   Bouillon™ Chicken Base
1 small onion, finely chopped
1/4 tsp poultry seasoning
1/2 tsp salt
1/2 tsp pepper
1/2 tsp garlic powder or 1
   clove garlic, finely
   chopped

1/2–3/4 cup olive or veg-
   etable oil
2 tsp Better Than Bouillon™
   Chicken Base
1 cup water

## GRAVY

1 tsp Better Than Bouillon™
   Chicken Base
2 cups cold water
1/2 cup flour

*Meatballs:* Mix all ingredients and form into balls by hand. Brown in skillet with oil. Add Better Than Bouillon™ Chicken Base and water to meatballs in skillet. Simmer on low heat for 10–15 minutes.

*Gravy:* In separate bowl, mix cold water, Better Than Bouillon™ Chicken Base, and flour with fork (until lumps are gone).

Pour gravy mixture into skillet with meatballs and cook over low-medium heat, stirring constantly. Bring to boil, then reduce heat to low and simmer, covered, for another 20–25 minutes. Serve over rice or egg noodles (recipe page vii).

# CHICKEN MARSALA

**Shirley Heublein**

*Use Beef Base*
*Servings: 4*

4 boneless, skinless chicken
   breasts, pounded
   1/4-inch thick
3 Tbs flour
1 1/2 teaspoons pepper
4 Tbs butter
1 Tbs vegetable oil
1/2 cup chopped onions
2 cloves garlic, minced
1/2 lb sliced mushrooms
2/3 tsp Better Than
   Bouillon™ Beef Base
   dissolved in 2/3 cups
   hot water
2/3 cups dry Marsala wine

Combine flour and pepper. Dredge chicken in flour mixture and shake off excess. Heat butter and oil in skillet over medium heat. Add chicken and cook 3 minutes on each side. Remove from pan. Add onion and garlic and sauté for 3 minutes. Add mushrooms and cook 3–5 minutes. Return chicken to skillet. Add Better Than Bouillon™ Beef Broth and Marsala. Bring to a boil and reduce heat. Simmer until liquid is reduced to 1/3. Serve with angel hair pasta with pesto sauce.

# "BETTER THAN BOUILLON" CHICKEN

**Therese Casavant**

*Use Chicken or Vegetable Base*
*Servings: 6*

1 3–4 lb chicken
Juice of one lemon
2 tsp celery salt
1 tsp rosemary
1 tsp paprika
1/2 cup olive oil
1 Tbs Better Than Bouillon™
   Chicken or Vegetable
   Base dissolved in
   2 Tbs warm water

Cut chicken along breast bone. Rinse well and sprinkle inside with lemon juice. Place chicken bone side down and flatten. Place chicken on rack in shallow roasting pan with bone-side down. Combine rest of ingredients and pour over chicken. Bake, uncovered, at 450° for 45–50 minutes, basting every 15 minutes, until browned. Reduce heat to 325° and bake, uncovered, for 30 minutes longer.

## MARDI GRAS CHICKEN

**Denise B. Penn**

*Use Chicken Base*
*Servings: 4*

2 Tbs olive oil
1/2 cup julienne red bell
    pepper
1/2 cup julienne green bell
    pepper
1/2 cup thinly sliced onion
4 boneless, skinless chicken
    breasts
1 cup uncooked converted
    rice
1/2 cup seedless raisins
2 tsp Better Than Bouillon™
    Chicken Base dissolved
    in 2 cups hot water
1/2 tsp chili powder
1/2 tsp paprika
1/4 tsp salt

Heat olive oil in heavy skillet over medium heat. Add peppers and onions, sauté until onions are soft. Remove from skillet and set aside.

Add chicken breasts and brown lightly, turning once. Remove from skillet and set aside. Add remaining ingredients to skillet and heat to boiling. Add peppers and onions to skillet evenly on top of liquid —*do not stir.* Lay chicken breasts on top of vegetables, allowing them to sink into hot liquid. Cover tightly, reduce heat, and simmer for 20 minutes, or until liquid is absorbed.

## CHICKEN A LA KING

**Superior Touch**

*Use Chicken Base*
*Servings: 4*

5 Tbs butter or margarine
1/2 cup flour
2 Tbs Better Than Bouillon™
    Chicken Base
2 cups milk
1/8 tsp pepper
1 4-oz can mushroom stems
    and pieces, undrained
1 8–10-oz box frozen peas
1 12-oz can or 1 1/2 cups
    cooked chicken, diced

Cooked noodles or rice

Melt butter in saucepan; remove from heat add stir in flour and Better Than Bouillon™ Chicken Base. Add milk, pepper and mushrooms (including liquid). Bring to boil. Add peas and chicken and simmer, covered, for 10 minutes. Serve over cooked noodles or rice (recipe page vii).

# FRENCH COUNTRY CHICKEN

**Margaret Ayton**

*Use Chicken and Beef Bases*
*Servings: 4*

*1 head garlic, cloves separat-*
*ed, but not peeled*
*4 skinless chicken breasts*
*Salt and pepper*
*2 tsp margarine or light*
*butter*
*1/2 cup red wine vinegar*
*2 cups water*
*1 1/2 tsp Better Than*
*Bouillon™ Chicken Base*
*1/2 tsp Better Than*
*Bouillon™ Beef Base*
*2 Tbs margarine or light*
*butter*
*4 medium tomatoes, diced*

Preheat oven to 375°. Peel 2 garlic cloves and rub into chicken breasts. Season chicken with salt and pepper. Melt 2 tsp margarine in skillet over medium-high heat. Add chicken and brown well on both sides. Transfer chicken to a baking pan. Add unpeeled garlic cloves and bake until chicken is cooked through (approximately 40 minutes).

Meanwhile, add vinegar to skillet and bring to a boil, scraping up any browned bits. Cook over medium heat until reduced to 2 Tbs (about 3 minutes). Add water and bring to a boil. Stir in Better Than Bouillon™ Chicken and Beef Bases. Continue boiling until reduced to 1/2 cup (about 20 minutes). Whisk in 2 Tbs margarine. Add tomatoes and stir until just heated through.

Place chicken on dinner plates or serving platter. Press garlic from skins onto chicken. Pour sauce over chicken and serve.

# LEMON CHICKEN WITH
# EGG AND SPINACH NOODLES

*Use Chicken Base*

## Sally L. Briceno

*Servings: 8*

2 broiler-fryer chickens,
    quartered
1/2 cup all-purpose flour
2 tsp salt
1/4 tsp pepper

1/3 cup vegetable oil
1 large onion, chopped
2 cloves garlic, minced
2 tsp Better Than Bouillon™
    Chicken Base dissolved
    in 2 cups hot water
1/2 cup lemon juice
Lemon slices
Black ripe olives

## N O O D L E S

1 8-oz pkg egg noodles
1 8 oz pkg spinach noodles
Salt
2 Tbs butter or margarine
1/2 tsp Better Than
    Bouillon™ Chicken Base
Freshly ground pepper

## S A U C E

1 egg
1/2 cup cold water
Salt and pepper, to taste
Lemon juice, to taste

Combine flour, salt and pepper in a plastic bag. Shake chicken quarters in bag, one at a time to coat evenly with mixture. Heat oil in a large skillet and brown chicken on all sides. Remove chicken. Pour off all but 2 Tbs of the pan drippings, and sauté onion and garlic until soft. Stir in Better Than Bouillon™ Chicken Broth and lemon juice until well-blended. Return chicken, skin side up, to skillet. Pour some sauce over chicken, cover skillet, and reduce heat. Simmer 30 minutes, or until chicken is fully cooked. While chicken is cooking, prepare noodles (as directed below).

Following package directions, cook egg and spinach noodles in a large kettle of boiling, salted water. Drain noodles and return to kettle. Toss noodles with butter, sprinkle with pepper, and toss. Place noodles on a platter and arrange chicken on top. Garnish with lemon slices and olives, and cover to keep hot while preparing sauce.

Beat egg with cold water in a bowl. Mix in one cup of the hot sauce until mixture is smooth. Stir mixture into skillet and heat, stirring constantly. Season to taste with salt, pepper and lemon juice. Spoon part of the sauce over chicken and serve remainder in a sauce boat at the table.

# FRAN'S LOW-FAT TURKEY CHILI

**Frances Cipriano**

*Use Chicken Base*
*Servings: 8*

2 lbs ground turkey
1/2 cup each red and green
    bell pepper, diced
1 1/2 Tbs chopped garlic
1 large onion, diced
Canola oil
2 Tbs chili powder
2 Tbs ground cumin
1/4 tsp oregano
1 1/2 Tbs Better Than
    Bouillon™ Chicken Base
1 28-oz can whole tomatoes,
    processed in blender
    (including juice)
2–3 cups water (or 2 cups
    water and 1 cup
    Chardonnay)
1/4 tsp sugar, or to taste
1 can baked black beans
3 canned chipotle chilies,
    seeded and chopped fine
Pepper, to taste
Tabasco or habenaro sauce,
    to taste

Sauté ground turkey, one pound at a time, in large skillet. Sauté all vegetables in oil and add to cooked turkey. Stir in chili powder, cumin, oregano, Better Than Bouillon™ Chicken Base, and processed tomatoes. Add water or water/wine mixture and sugar to taste. Bring to a boil and simmer for 20 minutes. Add black beans, chilies, and Tabasco sauce. Simmer 10 more minutes. Add pepper and Tabasco or habenaro sauce to taste. Serve with oyster crackers or corn bread.

# SHRIMP CREOLE

**Valerie Ferguson**

*Use Chili Base*
*Servings: 4*

1 small green bell pepper,
    chopped
1 small brown onion,
    chopped
2 stalks celery, chopped
2 Tbs olive oil
1 8-oz can tomato sauce
1 28-oz can crushed
    tomatoes
1 tsp salt
1 tsp pepper
1 Tbs garlic powder
1 Tbs basil
1 Tbs gumbo filet
2 Tbs Better Than Bouillon™
    Chili Base
1/2 cup water
1 1/2 lbs large shrimp,
    cleaned

In large pot, sauté bell pepper, onion and celery in olive oil. Add tomatoes, tomato sauce, spices, Better Than Bouillon™ Chili Base, and water. Simmer one hour and add shrimp. Serve over rice (recipe page vii).

# DILLED ALMOND TROUT

**Elaine Kennedy**

*Use Vegetable Base*
*Servings: 2*

2 10-oz trout
1/8 tsp black pepper
1/2 tsp dill weed
3/4 tsp Better Than
    Bouillon™ Vegetable
    Base
1/2 cup hot water
1/3 cup slivered almonds
Lemon wedges

Place cleaned trout in shallow baking dish. Mix pepper, dill and Better Than Bouillon™ Vegetable Base in water. Pour mixture over trout. Sprinkle almonds over fish and bake at 350° for 20–25 minutes, or until fish flakes when touched with fork. Season to taste with lemon and serve.

# SCALLOP STUFFIN' BAKE

**Doris Eberhardt**

*Use Chicken Base*
*Servings: 6*

2 cups fresh scallops, cut
    into bite-sized pieces
1/4 cup margarine or butter
1/2 cup chopped celery
1 medium onion, minced
1 large carrot, minced
1/4 cup flour
2 1/2 tsp Better Than
    Bouillon™ Chicken Base
1 1/2 cups water
3/4 cup milk
1 tsp chopped fresh parsley
1/4 cup grated parmesan
    cheese
1 7-oz package seasoned,
    cubed bread stuffing
1/4 cup finely chopped
    hazelnuts
1/2 cup shredded cheddar
    cheese
Sweet paprika

In a large saucepan, melt margarine and cook scallops over medium heat until scallops just turn white. Do not overcook. Remove from pan and set aside. Add celery, onion, and carrot, and sauté until tender. Add flour. Cook and stir for one minute. Combine Better Than Bouillon™ Chicken Base with water, milk, parsley, and parmesan cheese. Stir into vegetable mix. Bring mixture to a boil, stirring constantly. Reduce heat and continue to cook until thickened. Add bread cubes and nuts and toss to coat.

Place in a 2-qt baking dish and bake at 350° for 25 minutes. Remove from oven and add scallops. Return to oven for another 5 minutes. Remove from oven and sprinkle with cheddar cheese, topping with a dash of paprika over the top. Return to oven and bake another 5 minutes, or until cheese is melted.

# ELAINE'S GOOD STUFF PAELLA

**Elaine Marsilio**

*Use Chicken Base*
*Servings: 8–10*

6 links (1 1/4 lbs) hot Italian
   sausage
7 (1 1/2 lbs) boneless, skinless chicken thighs, cut
   into 3/4-inch slices
2 cups sliced fresh green
   onions
4 cloves garlic, crushed
1/2 tsp oregano
5 tsp Better Than Bouillon™
   Chicken Base
2 cups uncooked long-grain
   rice
6 cups water
3/4 tsp saffron threads
3 bay leaves
1/4 cup drained pimiento
5 Tbs freshly snipped parsley
3/4 lbs medium shrimp,
   deveined and peeled

Pierce sausage with fork and place in microwave-safe covered casserole with 1/2 inch of water. Microwave on high for 5 minutes, or until centers of sausages lose their pinkness. Drain and cut into 3/4-inch slices.

Place sausage and chicken in a 4-qt, non-stick Dutch oven. Brown over medium heat, stirring occasionally. Add onions, garlic, and oregano, cooking until meat is browned. Add Better Than Bouillon™ Chicken Base and uncooked rice, stirring to coat and blend all ingredients. Slowly stir in water. Add saffron and bay leaves. Bring to a boil, cover, and reduce heat. Simmer for 25–30 minutes. Add pimiento, parsley, and shrimp. Simmer for 10 minutes or until shrimp is cooked and rice is tender.

# BROWN-SEARED SEA SCALLOPS WITH MASHED CORN POTATOES AND RED EYE GRAVY

*Use Chicken and Beef Bases*
*Servings: 4*

## Thomas Hozduk

### SCALLOPS

16 large sea scallops
2 Tbs olive oil
2 shallots, chopped
1/2 cup fresh strong coffee
1 tsp Better Than Bouillon™
    Chicken Base and
1 tsp Better Than Bouillon™
    Beef Base dissolved in 2
    cups hot water
Fresh lemon juice, to taste
Fresh ground pepper, to taste

### POTATOES

3 large russet potatoes,
    peeled and cut into even
    chunks
2 Tbs olive oil
5 whole garlic cloves
1 cup half and half
2 tsp finely chopped fresh
    thyme
2 Tbs unsalted butter
White pepper, to taste
Kernels from 2 ears cooked
    sweet corn

Boil chopped potatoes in salted water until tender (about 30 minutes). While potatoes are cooking, heat oil over medium-low heat and sauté garlic until golden brown (about 10 minutes). Combine drained garlic, half and half, and thyme in food processor and blend until mixture is smooth. Drain cooked potatoes and place in mixing bowl with butter and half-and-half mixture. Whip potatoes with electric mixer until smooth. Add corn kernels and blend by hand. Season to taste with white pepper and keep warm.

Heat oil in large skillet over medium-high heat. Place scallops in skillet one by one. Sear scallops until brown, but not blackened (about 4–5 minutes, depending on the heat). Turn each scallop over and brown other side, being careful not to overcook. When done, remove scallops to covered dish. Reduce skillet to medium heat and add shallots, scraping bottom of pan with wooden spoon to remove brown bits. Add coffee and cook mixture until pan is dry (about 5 minutes). Add Better Than Bouillon™ Chicken and Beef Broth, as well as juices that have collected in dish with scallops. Reduce mixture by half. Season to taste.

Mound potatoes on plate and cover with 4 scallops. Spoon gravy over each scallop. Top with freshly ground pepper.

# BROILED LOBSTER
**Superior Touch**

*Use Lobster Base*
*Servings: 4*

*4 live lobsters, 1–2 lbs each*

L O B S T E R
B U T T E R

*1 Tbs Better Than Bouillon™*
*Lobster Base dissolved*
*in 1/4 lb melted butter*

*1 Tbs lemon juice*

Wash lobsters under cold water. Then, either plunge them head first into boiling water for 2 minutes, or insert a sharp knife through the cross at the back of the head. Cut the under side of lobster from head to tail. Remove the stomach (sac in back of head) and the intestinal vein that runs from the stomach to the tail. Broil about 5 inches from heat for 15 minutes. Serve with Better Than Bouillon™ Lobster Butter and lemon juice for dipping.

# BOILED LOBSTER
**Superior Touch**

*Use Lobster Base*
*Servings: 4*

*4 live lobsters, 1–2 lbs each*
*4 Tbs Better Than Bouillon™*
*Lobster Base*
*4 qts water*
*1/4 lb butter, melted*

Bring Better Than Bouillon™ Lobster Base and water to a boil in a large pot.

Wash lobsters under cold water. Plunge lobsters, head-first into pot. Cover and bring to a boil. Reduce heat and simmer 1-lb lobsters for 15 minutes; 2-lb lobsters for 20 minutes; larger lobsters for 30 minutes.

Remove and place in sink until cool enough to handle. Place lobster on its back and cut in half from head to tail. Remove stomach and intestinal vein. Serve with melted butter.

# FISH IN ITALIAN TOMATO SAUCE

**B. Caughman**

*Use Clam Base*
*Servings: 4*

1 medium onion, chopped
1/4 medium green pepper,
    chopped
1 clove garlic, minced
1 Tbs olive oil
1 16-oz can diced tomatoes
1/2 tsp dried oregano
1/2 tsp dried basil
1/4 tsp sugar, or to taste
1 lb fresh fish fillets or steaks
1/3 tsp Better Than
    Bouillon™ Clam Base
    dissolved in 1/3 cup
    water

2 Tbs cold water
1 Tbs cornstarch
2 Tbs grated romano cheese

Sauté onion, green pepper and garlic in hot olive oil over medium-high heat for 4–5 minutes or until tender but not brown. Stir in undrained tomatoes, oregano, basil and sugar. Bring to a boil. Reduce heat and simmer, covered, 20 minutes, stirring occasionally.

Cut fish fillets or steaks into 4 serving-size portions; rinse. Measure thickness of fish. Stir Better Than Bouillon™ Clam Broth into tomato mixture. Return to boiling; add fish. Spoon some tomato mixture over fish.

Return to boiling. Reduce heat; simmer, covered until fish flakes easily with a fork. Allow 4–6 minutes for each 1/2-inch of thickness. Transfer fish to a serving platter, reserving tomato mixture; keep fish warm.

Combine cold water and cornstarch and stir into tomato mixture to thicken. Cook over medium heat until bubbly. To serve, spoon sauce over fish and sprinkle with romano cheese.

## LOBSTER NEWBURG

**Superior Touch**

*Use Lobster Base*
*Servings: 4*

2 cups cooked lobster meat
3 Tbs butter
1/2 tsp Better Than
    Bouillon™ Lobster Base
3 Tbs flour
Pepper, to taste
1 1/2 cups milk
1 egg yolk, slightly beaten
1 1/2 Tbs sherry
1/4 lb mushrooms, sliced
    and sautéed in 2 Tbs
    butter for 3 minutes

2 Tbs chopped parsley

Melt butter and Better Than Bouillon™ Lobster Base over low heat. Add flour and pepper and stir one minute (until bubbly). Remove from heat and stir in milk. Return to heat, stirring until mixture reaches a boil. Combine half of the sauce with the egg yolk. Return mixture to saucepan, stirring as you pour. Add sherry, lobster meat and mushrooms. Heat and serve garnished with parsley.

## SAUTÉED SOFT-SHELLED CRABS

**Superior Touch**

*Use Lobster Base*
*Servings: 4*

8 soft-shelled crabs, cleaned
Salt and pepper
1 egg, slightly beaten
2/3 cup flour
1/3 cup bread crumbs
1/2 tsp Better Than
    Bouillon™ Lobster Base
3–6 Tbs butter

Preheat oven to 200°. Wash crabs and pat dry. Sprinkle with salt and pepper. Dip in egg and coat with a mixture of flour and bread crumbs. Sauté crabs in Better Than Bouillon™ Lobster Base and butter over medium heat, a few at a time, about 4 minutes per side. Add additional butter as needed. Remove crabs and keep warm in oven until all have been cooked. Excellent served on toast.

# NOTES

# NOTES

# NOTES

# NOTES

# NOTES

# NOTES

# BREADS, RICE & PASTA

*G*rains such as rice and wheat are very low in fat,
sugar and sodium and high in complex carbohydrates and fiber.
Better Than Bouillon™ can add subtle flavor to recipes in this
important food group, without adding extra fat or excessive salt.
For additional nutritional benefits, try using whole-grain flours
and pastas in place of refined products when possible. Unless
otherwise noted, please refer to product packaging for proper
cooking times for pasta.

# PIGS IN A BLANKET

**Robert Hamilton**

*Use Beef Base*
*Servings: 10*

1 lb small beef sausages or
    franks
2 Tbs water

## BATTER

3 cups all-purpose flour
1 tsp salt
1 tsp baking powder
6 eggs
2 1/2 cups milk

1/2 cup melted margarine
1 Tbs Better Than Bouillon™
    Beef Base

Preheat oven to 400°. Place sausages or franks side-by-side in a 10-12 inch skillet, and prick them with the tines of a fork. Sprinkle with 2 Tbs water, cover tightly, and cook over low heat for 3 minutes. Remove cover and increase heat to moderate. Continue to cook, turning the sausages frequently, until water has completely evaporated and sausages have begun to brown. Remove from skillet and set aside.

Combine flour, salt and baking powder in a mixing bowl. In a larger bowl, beat eggs with mixer on low speed for 30 seconds. Add milk and beat 15 seconds more. Add flour mixture and beat on low speed 2 minutes or until smooth.

Place melted margarine in a 15-1/2x10-1/2x2 inch roasting pan or a 10-12 inch cast iron skillet. Stir in Better Than Bouillon™ Beef Base and heat until mixture is almost to the point of burning. Spoon batter mixture into pan or skillet and arrange sausages on top of batter, keeping them at least one inch apart. Bake in upper half of oven for 30 minutes. Serve at once.

# MASHED POTATO BREAD
**Superior Touch**

*Use Chicken or Vegetable Base*
*Yield: 1 loaf*

*8 cups flour*
*2 1/4-oz pkgs active dry*
*yeast*
*1 1/4 cups tepid milk*
*2 tsp Better Than Bouillon™*
*Chicken or Vegetable*
*Base dissolved in*
*1 1/4 cups tepid water*
*1 tsp salt*
*4 medium-sized potatoes,*
*boiled, peeled and*
*mashed (about 2 cups)*

Mix yeast with 1/2 cup of the tepid milk. Sift 8 cups of flour together with the salt into a bowl. Rub the mashed potatoes into the flour, as if rubbing in fat, to make a smooth mixture. Add more flour if needed. Work in the yeast mixture and the rest of the milk and Better Than Bouillon™ Chicken or Vegetable Broth. Knead thoroughly and let the dough rise until doubled in bulk—about 2 hours.

Punch down the dough and knead it lightly. Lay it on a floured baking sheet and shape it into a round or oval loaf. Cover the loaf with a damp cloth and let it rise for about 30 minutes, or until it has increased in bulk by half. Bake the loaf in a preheated 425° oven for about 45 minutes, or until the crust is light brown.

# CHRIS' CHORIZO SAUSAGE TURKEY STUFFING

**Chris Bjornstedt**

*Use Beef Base*
*Servings: 6*

*1 lb chorizo sausage, skin removed*
*1 each green, red, and yellow bell pepper, finely chopped*
*2 stalks celery, finely chopped*
*1 6-oz pkg seasoned dressing*
*1 tsp Better Than Bouillon™ Beef Base dissolved in 2/3 cups hot water*

Brown sausage in large skillet, crumbling sausage as it cooks. Add peppers and celery and cook, stirring occasionally, for about 10 minutes. Drain sausage to remove as much fat as possible. Place seasoned dressing in large bowl and add meat and vegetables. Add Better Than Bouillon™ Beef Broth and place in a greased, covered casserole. Bake in 350° oven for 35 minutes. Remove cover and bake an additional 10 minutes for a crispy top. Alternatively, refrigerate uncooked stuffing until ready to stuff turkey. Recipe is adequate for a 10-lb turkey.

# PEPPER CHEESE LOAF

**Rebecca Coleman**

*Use Chicken or Vegetable Base*
*Yield: 2 loaves*

*2 1/2-3 cups all-purpose flour*
*1/4 oz pkg active dry yeast*
*2 Tbs sugar*
*1 tsp salt*
*2 tsp freshly ground black pepper*
*1/2 tsp Better Than Bouillon™ Chicken or Vegetable Base dissolved in 1 cup tepid water*
*1 Tbs vegetable oil*
*2 cups coarsely grated sharp cheddar cheese*

In a mixer bowl blend one cup flour, yeast, sugar, salt, and pepper. Add Better Than Bouillon™ Chicken or Vegetable Broth and oil. Beat with an electric mixer at low speed for 30 seconds, scraping bowl once or twice. Then, at high speed, beat for 3 minutes. With a wooden spoon, stir in additional flour, 1/2 cup at a time, to form a soft dough that is elastic. Turn out on a floured work surface and knead for about five minutes. Place dough in a lightly greased bowl, cover and set in a warm place until the dough has doubled in bulk. Punch down the dough, working out the bubbles. Spread half of the cheese on the dough and fold it in. Knead for one minute. Sprinkle the rest of the cheese on dough and continue kneading until it has been absorbed by the dough.

With a sharp knife, divide dough in half. Shape the pieces into balls; allow to rise under a towel for 3–4 minutes. Press each ball of dough into a greased one-pound coffee can. One ball should fill a coffee can no more than half-way. Loaf pans may be used. Place containers in a warm place and let dough rise. Bake in a preheated 400° oven 30–35 minutes or until loaves sound hollow. Cool on wire racks.

# SAGE FLATBREAD
**Superior Touch**

*Use Vegetable Base*
*Yield: 1 loaf*

*2 1/2 cups flour*
*1/4-oz pkg active dry yeast*
*1/2 tsp Better Than*
*    Bouillon™ Vegetable*
*    Base dissolved in*
*    1 cup tepid water*
*1 Tbs olive oil*
*3 large fresh sage leaves,*
*    center ribs removed and*
*    coarsely chopped*
*1 egg yolk*
*Sea salt*

Mix yeast with the Better Than Bouillon™ Vegetable Broth. Add chopped sage leaves and olive oil, then work in the flour until dough is firm enough to be turned out on a floured surface. Continue adding flour until dough pulls away from your hand as you knead and no longer sticks to the work surface. Knead hard for 10-12 minutes. Let the dough double in bulk—at least 40 minutes.

Roll dough into a round approximately one-inch thick. Place dough on an oiled baking sheet and make a series of indentations in the dough with a finger. Brush dough with egg-yolk glaze and, in the center, place the sprig of sage to decorate the bread. Sprinkle bread with a small handful of sea salt and allow to rise 40 minutes. Bake bread in a preheated 375° oven for about 45 minutes.

# CORNMEAL STICKS

**(Surullitos)**

**Chef Jorge Bruce**

*Use Chicken Base*
*Servings: 6–8*

1 cup water
1 tsp Better Than Bouillon™ Chicken Base
2/3 tsp salt
2 tsp unsalted butter
1 1/4 cup coarsely ground yellow cornmeal
1/3 cup grated edam cheese
Vegetable or canola oil for frying

Combine water, Better Than Bouillon™ Chicken Base, salt, and butter in a large pot and bring to a boil. In a separate bowl, combine cornmeal and cheese. Remove boiling water from heat and rapidly stir in cornmeal mixture. If the mixture is too dry, add water.

Roll one Tbs of mixture at a time into balls. Shape balls into cylinders (the shape of small cigars).

Heat oil in deep skillet. Fry one layer at a time until golden brown. Drain on absorbent paper.

Serve with stewed beans as a side dish (recipe page 152).

# TORTAS

**Chef Jorge Bruce**

*Use Chicken Base*
*Servings: 6–8*

2 cups flour
1/4 tsp Better Than Bouillon™ Chicken Base dissolved in 1 cup water
1/4 tsp salt
1 tsp vegetable oil

Vegetable or canola oil for frying

Mix flour, Better Than Bouillon™ Chicken Broth, salt and one tsp vegetable oil into a dough. Form 1 1/2-inch diameter balls. Flatten balls to 1/4-inch thick cakes.

Heat oil in heavy skillet. Fry single layer one side at a time until golden brown. Drain.

Excellent with stewed beans (recipe page 152), dip, or salsa.

# BASIC "BETTER THAN BOUILLON" BREAD DOUGH

**Superior Touch**

*Use Any Base*
*Yield: 2 loaves or 30 rolls*

*Approximately 6 cups flour*
*1/4 oz pkg active dry yeast*
*or 3/5-oz cake fresh*
*yeast*
*1 tsp salt*
*1 tsp Better Than Bouillon™*
*Base\**
*Approximately 2 cups tepid*
*water*

*\* Any of the six Better Than*
*Bouillon™ Bases*
*(Chicken, Beef,*
*Vegetable, Clam,*
*Lobster, or Chili) may be*
*used*

Proof the yeast in about 1/4 cup of the tepid water (approximately 110°) by letting it stand for 10 minutes. Sift flour and salt into a large bowl. Dissolve Better Than Bouillon™ Chicken Base into remaining water. Pour yeast mixture and Better Than Bouillon™ Broth into the flour. Mix flour and liquid together into a stiff, sticky dough, adding more flour or tepid water if necessary. Transfer dough to a work surface and knead for about 15 minutes, until it is elastic and glossy.

Shape dough into a ball and place into a greased bowl. Cover bowl and let rise in a warm, draft-free location until doubled in volume (1–2 1/2 hours). Dough is ready when the insertion of a finger leaves a dent that does not immediately smooth out.

Punch dough down. Place dough on a work surface and cut it in half. Knead each half into a ball, cover balls with a cloth, and let them rise for 10–15 minutes. The dough is now ready for shaping and baking as described in the following recipes.

# WALNUT AND ONION BREAD
**Superior Touch**

*Use Chicken or Vegetable Base*
*Yield: 1 loaf*

*1/2 Basic Better Than Bouillon™ Bread Dough (see page 122)*
*2 small onions, sliced into thick rounds*
*Salt and pepper, to taste*
*2-3 Tbs walnut oil*
*2-3 Tbs finely chopped walnuts*

Prepare Basic Better Than Bouillon™ Bread Dough. After the first rise, punch dough down and divide into two pieces, one twice as big as the other. Roll out the larger piece in a circle about 3/4-inch thick to fit a round or square baking sheet. Place dough on buttered baking sheet.

Divide remaining dough into 5–6 pieces and roll them into sausage shapes, each about the thickness of a finger. Bend these pieces of dough into 2-inch rings, pinching the ends firmly together. Arrange the rings on top of the dough on the baking sheet. Lay an onion round in the center of each dough ring, and arrange the remaining onion rounds over the rest of the rolled-out dough. Cover bread and allow to rise for about one hour. Season the bread with salt and pepper, sprinkle with oil and scatter the walnuts over the surface. Bake in a preheated 350°F oven for about 40 minutes, or until bread sounds slightly hollow when rapped on the bottom. Allow to cool before serving.

# ITALIAN FLATBREAD WITH HAM
**Superior Touch**

*Use Chicken or Vegetable Base*
*Yield: 1 loaf*

*1/2 Basic Better Than
Bouillon Bread Dough
(see page 122)
1/4 lb prosciutto, diced
1/4 tsp Better Than
Bouillon™ Chicken or
Vegetable Base dissolved
in 1/4 cup water
2 tsp coarse salt*

Prepare Basic Better Than Bouillon™ Bread Dough. After the first rise, knead in prosciutto and Better Than Bouillon™ Chicken or Vegetable Broth. The dough will be rather soft. Roll dough into a round about 3/4-inch thick and lay it on a buttered baking sheet. With a sharp knife, lightly score the surface to create a lattice pattern. Sprinkle dough with coarse salt. Allow dough to rise in a warm place for 20 minutes. Bake in a preheated 425° oven for about 20 minutes, or until brown. Serve bread while still warm.


# AUTHENTIC SPANISH RICE
**Barbara Cosio**

*Use Chicken Base*
*Servings: 4*

*1 cup long-grain white rice
1/4-1/2 small onion, finely
chopped
Canola oil
2 Tbs Better Than Bouillon™
Chicken Base dissolved
in 2 1/2 cups hot water
4 oz tomato sauce
Garlic
Better Than Bouillon™
Chicken Base to taste*

Sauté rice and onion in hot oil until golden brown. Add Better Than Bouillon™ Chicken Broth, tomato sauce, salt, and a pinch of garlic to browned rice and onion mixture. Stir and cover pan. Cook over low heat until water evaporates (approximately 20 minutes).

*Variation:* Add 1/4 cup finely chopped cooked carrots and 1/4 cup cooked green peas.

# GREEN RICE

**Nancy Rommelmann**

*Use Chicken Base*
*Servings: 6–8*

4 cups water
2 Tbs Better Than Bouillon™
  Chicken Base
4 Tbs butter
1 bunch scallions, chopped
1 bunch Italian (flat leaf)
  parsley, chopped
1 pkg frozen chopped
  spinach, cooked and
  squeezed dry
2 cups uncooked rice

Boil water and add Better Than Bouillon™ Chicken Base. Stir until dissolved and remove from heat.

Melt butter in heavy saucepan. Add chopped scallions, parsley, and spinach, stirring until scallions are wilted and mixture is shiny and well blended. Add rice, stirring until coated. Continue to stir while adding stock. Bring to a boil, reduce heat and cover. Simmer 17–20 minutes, until rice is tender. Fluff with a fork.

# RED RICE

**Diane Calderon**

*Use Chicken Base*
*Servings: 4*

1 cup uncooked long-grain
  white rice
2 Tbs vegetable oil
1/2 medium tomato
2 cloves garlic, minced
2 cups water
1 1/2 Tbs Better Than
  Bouillon™ Chicken Base

Sauté rice in vegetable oil until it turns white. Blend tomato, garlic, Better Than Bouillon™ Chicken Base and water in blender or food processor. Add sautéed rice and cook over low heat for 20 minutes or until all moisture has been absorbed and rice is tender. Fluff rice with fork and serve.

For added color, add 1/4 cup frozen vegetable mix and bring to a boil before reducing heat. Simmer for 20 minutes, as above.

125

# INSTANT SEASONED MUSHROOM RICE

**Steve Kennedy**

*Use Chicken, Beef, or Vegetable Base*
*Servings: 4–6*

2 cups water
2 cups instant rice
1/2 cup freeze-dried mush-
    rooms
1/2 Tbs dried onions
1/2 tsp parsley
2 tsp Better Than Bouillon™
    Chicken, Beef, or
    Vegetable Base
Salt and pepper, to taste

Bring water to a boil and add rice, mushrooms, onions, parsley and Better Than Bouillon™ Base. Stir to moisten all ingredients. Remove from heat, cover tightly, and allow to steam for 5–7 minutes. Fluff with fork and serve.

# MEXICALI RICE

**Joanne Smith**

*Use Vegetable Base*
*Servings: 4–6*

3 tsp Better Than Bouillon™
    Vegetable Base dissolved
    in 2 1/2 cups hot water
1 onion, diced
1/2 red pepper, diced
3 stalks celery, cut on the
    diagonal
1 cup white long-grain rice
1 can whole kernel corn,
    drained
1/4 tsp pepper
1/4 tsp chili powder
2 large tomatoes, peeled and
    diced
1/4 cup fresh cilantro
Salt, to taste

Pour 1/2 cup of Better Than Bouillon™ Vegetable Broth into skillet and add onion, pepper and celery. Simmer for 5 minutes. Add rice, corn, pepper, chili, and remaining Better Than Bouillon™ Vegetable Broth. Cover and simmer slowly for 20 minutes, or until liquid has been absorbed. Stir once or twice during cooking. Add tomatoes and cilantro. Cover and cook about 2 minutes.

# PUERTO RICAN YELLOW RICE

**Chef Jorge Bruce**

*Use Chicken Base*
*Servings: 3–4*

*2 Tbs vegetable oil*
*1 tsp annato seeds*
*Pinch Bojo (can be found in the Spanish or Mexican food section)*
*1/2 tsp Better Than Bouillon™ Chicken Base dissolved in 2 cups water*
*1/2 small onion, diced*
*1/2 small tomato, diced*
*2 tsp small capers*
*6-8 stuffed olives*
*1 tsp salt*
*Pinch pepper*
*1 cup long-grain rice*

In a cast iron pot, slowly heat oil and annato seeds until seeds are black and oil is red. Remove from heat and discard seeds. Add small pinch Bojo; mix well. On high heat, add onions and tomatoes and gently sauté without burning. Add water, capers, olives, salt, and pepper. Bring to a boil, add rice. Boil until water level is 1/2-inch above rice, stirring occasionally. Reduce heat to medium low and simmer 3–5 minutes (or until most of the water is evaporated leaving a wet rice). Reduce heat to very low for another 15 minutes, stirring once or twice with a fork. Serve with stewed beans (recipe page 152).

*Note:* The bottom of the rice might turn a light brown. This "crunchy rice" is considered a delicacy called pegao. Carefully scrape the pegao off the bottom of the pot after the rest of the rice has been removed, and serve with the meal.

# RICE WITH BASIL AND PINE NUTS

**Mary Sue Storm**

*Use Chicken or Vegetable Base*
*Servings: 4*

2 Tbs unsalted butter
1 medium onion, chopped
   (Texas 1015, if avail-
   able)
1 cup basmati or jasmine rice
2 cups water
1 Tbs Better Than Bouillon™
   Chicken or Vegetable
   Base
1/3 cup toasted pine nuts
1/2 cup fresh basil, chopped

Heat water and Better Than Bouillon™ Chicken or Vegetable Base in microwave on high for 2 minutes. Add onion and sauté until soft (about 2 minutes). Stir to dissolve, set aside.

Melt butter in saucepan with tight-fitting lid over medium-high heat. Add onion and sauté until soft (about 2 minutes) Add rice and sauté one minute. Add Better Than Bouillon™ mixture and stir. Cover pan, reduce to medium heat, and simmer 15–20 minutes. Remove from heat and let stand 5 minutes. Fluff rice with fork, add pine nuts and basil, and serve.

# HEAVENLY CHICKEN RICE PILAF

**Rev. Carol Bolhuis**

*Use Chicken Base*
*Servings: 6*

1 cup chopped onion
1 cup chopped celery
1 tsp parsley
3 Tbs margarine or butter
1 cup long-grain rice
2 tsp Better Than Bouillon™
   Chicken Base dissolved
   in 2 cups hot water

Sauté onion, celery, parsley, rice, and butter in skillet until golden brown. Add Better Than Bouillon™ Chicken Broth, bring to a boil and allow to reduce, stirring occasionally. Cover, reduce heat to low, and simmer for 15–30 minutes.

# ANTE BELLUM BEANS AND RICE

**Ed Haas**

*Use Beef or Chicken Base*
*Servings: 4*

*1/2 pkg dried red kidney beans*
*1 Tbs Better Than Bouillon™ Beef or Chicken Base*
*1 cup rice*
*1 oz salt pork*
*1 onion, chopped*
*1 clove garlic, chopped*
*Tabasco sauce, to taste*

Place beans in Dutch oven and cover with water. Add Better Than Bouillon™ Beef or Chicken Base, cover, and simmer all day. Add water if necessary.

An hour before mealtime, prepare rice according to package instructions. Meanwhile, fry salt pork in skillet and discard. Sauté onion and garlic in drippings. Add onion, garlic, and some of the pan drippings to beans. Mound rice in bowls and ladle beans over rice and serve. Season to taste with a dash or two of Tabasco sauce.

*Variation:* Add 2 Tbs chopped bell pepper and one Tbs pimiento.

# COUSCOUS WITH PINE NUTS AND RAISINS

**Jeanne Moody**

*Use Chicken Base*
*Servings: 6*

*3/4 of a 5-oz box of couscous*
*1 Tbs butter*
*1 clove garlic, minced*
*1 1/2 tsp Better Than Bouillon™ Chicken Base dissolved in 1 cup hot water*
*1/4 cup toasted pine nuts or almonds*
*1/4 cup raisins, plumped in hot water and drained*

Sauté garlic in butter for 2 minutes. Add Better Than Bouillon™ Chicken Broth and bring to a boil. Stir in couscous and cover. Simmer for about 4 minutes, until couscous is tender. Fluff couscous while adding nuts and raisins.

# GOAT CHEESE PASTA

**Joan Weatherly**

*Use Chicken or Vegetable Base*
*Servings: 6*

*3 or 4 large shallots, minced*
*1 Tbs extra virgin olive oil*
*1 Tbs butter*
*6 tsp Better Than Bouillon™*
*Chicken or Vegetable*
*Base dissolved in*
*3 1/2 cups hot water*
*1 cup dry vermouth*
*1 lb chevre (goat cheese)*
*1 bunch Italian parsley,*
*chopped*
*Salt, to taste*
*Pepper, to taste*
*1 cup toasted pine nuts*
*1 lb angel hair pasta*

Sauté shallots in olive oil and butter until soft. Add Better Than Bouillon™ Chicken or Vegetable Broth to shallots. Add dry vermouth and bring to a simmer. Add goat cheese and simmer until melted. Simmer a few minutes to thicken a little. Add salt and pepper to taste.

Cook pasta as directed on package. Add to very hot sauce along with parsley. Toss to mix thoroughly and serve topped with pine nuts.

# FLORENTINE NOODLES

**Judith Rosenberg**

*Use Vegetable Base*
*Servings: 6*

*2 Tbs olive oil*
*1 large onion, sliced*
*2 cloves garlic, minced*
*1 10-oz package chopped*
*spinach, thawed*
*1 tsp basil*
*1/2 tsp salt or 1 1/2 tsp*
*Better Than Bouillon™*
*Vegetable Base*
*1/2 cup grated parmesan*
*cheese*
*1 lb spinach noodles, cooked*
*and drained*
*1 tsp Better Than Bouillon™*
*Vegetable Base dissolved*
*in 1 cup hot water*
*2 Tbs vinegar*

Sauté onion and garlic in oil for 5 minutes. Add spinach and Better Than Bouillon™ Vegetable Broth. Cover and cook 5 minutes on medium heat. Add basil and salt. Cover and cook 5 minutes. Add vinegar, cheese, and noodles. Top with additional parmesan cheese, if desired.

# ROASTED GARLIC LINGUINI FINI FLORENTINE

*Use Chicken Base*

Joyce E. Lynn

*Servings: 4–6*

### GARLIC

3–4 heads garlic, separated,
peeled, and trimmed
1/2 tsp olive oil
1 tsp Better Than Bouillon™
Chicken Base
2 Tbs white wine or water

### SAUCE

1 10-oz pkg frozen, chopped
spinach
1/4 cup chopped Italian
parsley
4 oz nonfat cream cheese,
cut into pieces
2 Tbs freshly grated parmesan cheese
1/2 tsp freshly cracked black
pepper
1 bunch green onions, finely
sliced
2 tsp Better Than Bouillon™
Chicken Base

### PASTA

1 lb linguini fini pasta,
cooked and drained
1 cup water from boiled
pasta

Place garlic in small microwave-safe dish and coat with olive oil. Add Better Than Bouillon™ Chicken Base and wine and microwave for 3 minutes. Stir to blend, and thoroughly coat garlic cloves with oil mixture. Roast in a 350° oven for about one hour, stirring several times. Check for doneness often toward the end. When done, the cloves should be very soft, piercing easily with a fork—just slightly shriveled, but not yet beginning to brown. Mash garlic thoroughly with a fork. If desired, mashed garlic can be refrigerated in a tightly covered container for up to two weeks.

Meanwhile, defrost and cook spinach in microwave in a large, covered microwave-safe bowl. Add Better Than Bouillon™ Chicken Base and parsley. Stir in mashed garlic (warmed, if it has been refrigerated) and cream cheese pieces. Stir until cheese has melted and no lumps of white remain. Add grated parmesan cheese, black pepper, and green onions. Toss with hot, drained pasta. Heat in microwave for a few minutes to help blend the flavors. If pasta seems too dry, add some of the pasta cooking water. Serve topped with grated parmesan cheese.

# ITALIAN VEGETABLE PASTA

**Ruth Scott**

*Use Beef, Chicken, or Vegetable Base*
*Servings: 4–6*

1/2 medium brown onion,
    minced
1 Tbs fresh minced garlic
1 Tbs olive oil
2 small crookneck yellow
    squash, cut into
    1/2-inch slices
1 medium zucchini, cut into
    1/2-inch slices
1 14-oz can stewed tomatoes
1/8 tsp pepper
3/4 tsp Better Than
    Bouillon™ Beef, Chicken,
    or Vegetable Base
1 tsp Italian seasoning
1-2 tsp brown sugar, to taste
10 oz mostaccioli, cooked,
    drained and rinsed (add
    1 tsp Better Than
    Bouillon™ Beef Base to
    cooking water for more
    flavor)
Grated parmesan and
    romano cheeses

Sauté onions and garlic in olive oil in a cast iron skillet until garlic is golden brown. Add remaining ingredients, except pasta and cheeses. Simmer for 20 minutes, or until vegetables are tender. Toss with pasta and garnish with cheeses. Serve immediately.

# TASTY CLAMS WITH PASTA

**Chef Jorge Bruce**

*Use Clam Base*
*Servings: 4*

4 doz littleneck or cherry-
    stone clams
4 cloves garlic, minced
3 Tbs olive oil
1/4 tsp Better Than
    Bouillon™ Clam Base
1/4 cup water

Sauté garlic in olive oil for 2 minutes. Add Better Than Bouillon™ Clam Base, water, and washed clams. Cover and bring to a boil. Lower heat and simmer 10-15 minutes or until shells open. Serve over hot pasta (recipe page vii).

# TRI-COLORED PASTA ITALIANA

**Jean MacDonald**

*Use Chicken Base*
*Servings: 4–6*

1 pkg multi-colored spiral
    pasta
3 Tbs olive oil
1/2 zucchini, sliced
1 cup chopped celery
1/2 red bell pepper, chopped
1/2 green bell pepper,
    chopped
1/2 brown onion, chopped
1 tsp chopped garlic
Salt, to taste
Pepper, to taste
Italian seasonings (oregano,
    basil, parsley), to taste
2 Tbs Better Than Bouillon™
    Chicken Base dissolved
    in 1 cup hot water
3 cooked chicken breasts
2 tsp walnut oil
2 tsp pine nuts
2 tsp capers

Sauté zucchini, celery, red and green bell pepper, onion, and garlic in olive oil. Add salt, pepper, and Italian herbs, to taste. When vegetables are half-cooked, add Better Than Bouillon™ Chicken Broth. Add chicken and simmer until vegetables are done. Drain pasta and sprinkle with walnut oil, pine nuts and capers. Serve hot or cold.

# BROCCOLI WITH PASTA

**Scott Kingsbury**

*Use Beef Base*
*Servings: 4*

1 Tbs finely chopped garlic
1/4 cup olive oil
1 head broccoli, cut into
    flowerettes
5 tsp Better Than Bouillon™
    Beef Base dissolved in
    6 cups hot water
1 lb pasta (ziti, mosticiolli, or
    rotini)
1/4 cup finely chopped fresh
    parsley
Parmesan cheese

Sauté garlic in oil briefly; do not brown. Add broccoli and sauté just until garlic browns. Add Better Than Bouillon™ Beef Broth and pasta and cook until pasta is al denté (slightly chewy). Mix in parsley and serve with parmesan cheese.

# FETTUCCINI WITH SUN DRIED TOMATOES AND MUSHROOMS

**Laurie Kircharik**

*Use Chicken Base*
*Servings: 4*

1/3 lb fettuccini
1 Tbs olive oil or margarine
1 small can (4-6 oz) sliced
  mushrooms (fresh
  mushrooms may be
  substituted)
1 tsp oregano
Salt and pepper, to taste
3/4 tsp Better Than
  Bouillon™ Chicken Base
  dissolved in 3/4 cup
  hot water
Grated fresh parmesan
  cheese
1 tsp tomato paste (optional)
1/2 cup chopped sun dried
  tomatoes

Boil pasta according to directions on package. While pasta is cooking, sauté mushrooms in olive oil or margarine 1–2 minutes. Add sun dried tomatoes, oregano, salt and pepper and heat through 1–2 minutes more. Add to mushroom mixture and continue to heat gently on low heat until pasta is cooked. Season to taste with salt and pepper. Drain pasta and spoon sauce over top. Sprinkle with parmesan cheese.

*Note:* For a thicker sauce, add tomato paste after adding Better Than Bouillon™ Chicken Broth.

# NOODLES IN OYSTER SAUCE

**Superior Touch**

*Use Chicken Base*
*Servings: 4*

1/2 lb narrow, flat Chinese
  egg noodles, cooked
1/4 cup peanut oil
1 walnut0sized piece ginger
  root, grated
3 scallions, sliced into 1-inch
  pieces
1/2 tsp Better Than
  Bouillon™ Chicken Base
  dissolved in 1/2 cup hot
  water
Oyster sauce

Heat oil over high heat; add ginger and scallions and stir fry briskly for two minutes. Add Better Than Bouillon™ Chicken Broth a little at a time, stirring constantly until the liquid all but disappears. Quickly add noodles and toss until smoking hot. (The noodles will be a bit shiny from the oil left in the pan.)

Serve with individual dip dishes of oyster sauce.

# NOTES

# NOTES

# NOTES

_____
_____
_____
_____
_____
_____
_____
_____
_____
_____
_____
_____
_____
_____
_____
_____
_____
_____
_____
_____
_____

# NOTES

# SALADS &
# VEGETABLES

$S$alads are one of today's most versatile courses.  They
may be served as a first course or entrée and presented hot or
cold.  Better Than Bouillon™ adds zest to salad dressings without
adding many calories.

$O$nce vegetables were the dreary accompaniment to
meat-based meals.  No longer true.  Vegetables are now highly
valued as meals in themselves.   For best taste and nutrition,
shop for vegetables that are in season.  Use the following Better
Than Bouillon™ recipes to liven up your palate and fulfill the
"5-a-day" plan for better health.

# CYNDEE'S POTATO SALAD

**Cyndee Masi**

*Use Chicken Base*
*Servings: 6*

3 cups potatoes, peeled and
  diced
1 tsp Better Than Bouillon™
  Chicken Base
1/2 tsp minced garlic
1/2 cup sliced carrots
1 egg

### D R E S S I N G

1/3 cup mayonnaise
2 tsp mustard
1 tsp Better Than Bouillon™
  Chicken Base
Salt, to taste
Pepper, to taste

1/2 cup chopped celery
1/2 cup chopped dill pickles
1 small jar pimientos

Fill a 2-qt saucepan with water
and bring to a boil. Add Better Than
Bouillon™ Chicken Base, potatoes,
garlic, carrots, and egg (in shell). Boil
for 7-10 minutes, or until potatoes
and carrots are soft and egg is hard-
boiled. Drain water and let cool.

Mix mayonnaise, mustard, Better
Than Bouillon™ Chicken Base, salt,
and pepper. Place potatoes and carrots in large bowl. Peel and chop egg
and add to mixture. Mix in celery,
pickle, and pimiento. Add dressing
and toss until well-blended. Serve
chilled.

# LIGHT BEAN SALAD

**Stephanie Michaels**

*Use Vegetable Base*
*Servings: 4*

1 9-oz pkg frozen french-
  style green beans,
  thawed
1 tsp Better Than Bouillon™
  Vegetable Base
1 medium carrot, finely
  chopped
2 Tbs finely chopped red
  onion
3 Tbs vinaigrette (recipe
  page 34)

Sauté green beans in Better Than
Bouillon™ Vegetable Base over low
heat until just cooked. Drain and
cool. Toss together beans, carrots,
onions and vinaigrette. Cover and
refrigerate at least 4 hours.

# CURRIED CHICKEN RICE SALAD

**Marlene Maher**

*Use Chicken Base*
*Servings: 6–8*

*1 box chicken-flavored Rice-
   A-Roni™*
*1/2 tsp Better Than
   Bouillon™ Chicken Base*
*Juice from marinated arti-
   choke hearts*
*3 large chicken breasts,
   cooked and diced*
*1/2 cup diced celery*
*1 small can sliced ripe olives,
   drained*
*6 scallions, thinly sliced*
*1 jar marinated artichoke
   hearts, chopped*
*1/2 cup sweet onion, diced*
*1/2 cup mayonnaise*
*1/2 tsp curry powder*
*Lettuce leaves*

Prepare Rice-A-Roni™ as directed and cool. Combine Better Than Bouillon™ Chicken Base with juice from marinated artichoke hearts. In a large bowl, combine rice, chicken, celery, olives, scallions, artichoke hearts, and onion. Add mayonnaise, curry powder, and artichoke juice mixture. Chill and serve on a bed of lettuce.

# CHICKEN SALAD

**Marcia Tonner**

*Use Chicken Base*
*Servings: 6–8*

DRESSING

*3/4 cup mayonnaise*
*1/2 cup drained plain yogurt*
*2 Tbs minced onion*
*1 Tbs parsley*
*2 Tbs lemon juice*
*1 Tbs Better Than Bouillon™
   Chicken Base*

*4 cups cooked chicken, cubed*
*1/2 cup chopped celery*
*2 medium apples, cubed*
*Mixed salad greens*

*Dressing:* Mix all ingredients and chill.

Toss chicken, celery and apples together with dressing until coated. Serve on mixed salad greens or toss dressing and mixed greens with chicken, celery and apples. Ideal as a side dish or main meal.

## "QUICK-FIX" SALAD

**Mary Anne Humphreys**

*Use Vegetable Base*
*Servings: 4–5*

*1/2 tsp Better Than
   Bouillon™ Vegetable
   Base dissolved in
   1/2 cup hot water*
*1/4 tsp dried oregano,
   crushed*
*1/2 small head (approx 3
   cups) cabbage, shredded*
*3 medium carrots, shredded
   (approx 1 cup)*
*1 medium onion, thinly sliced
   (approx 1/2 cup)*

Combine all ingredients in skillet and simmer over low heat for 15 minutes or until vegetables are tender, stirring occasionally. Drain before serving. Can be main entrée or side dish. Great with hot bread.


## CHICKEN STIR-FRY WITH SALAD

**Victoria Taylor**

*Use Chicken Base*
*Servings: 3–4*

*2–3 carrots, chopped*
*1 onion, chopped*
*1 small cabbage*
*4–5 Chinese snow peas*
*2 tsp canola oil*
*1/3 tsp Better Than
   Bouillon™ Chicken Base
   dissolved in 1/3 cup
   hot water*
*1–2 boneless chicken breasts,
   cubed*
*2 Tbs light soy sauce*
*1 tsp Tabasco sauce*
*2 Tbs Chinese red garlic
   sauce*
*1 small head lettuce*
*1 large tomato*

Stir-fry carrots, onion, cabbage and peas in canola oil until tender. Remove from pan and drain. Place Better Than Bouillon™ Chicken Broth and chicken in pan and sauté until meat is cooked. Add cooked vegetables, soy sauce, Tabasco sauce, and red garlic sauce. Sauté until vegetables are heated. Layer lettuce and tomatoes on plate, top with stir-fried vegetables and serve.

# HOT GERMAN POTATO SALAD

**Superior Touch**

*Use Beef Base*
*Servings: 5–6*

*5 medium russet potatoes*
*1 tsp Better Than Bouillon™*
*Beef Base per 1 cup*
*water for boiling pota-*
*toes*
*1/2 lb bacon, diced*
*1 Tbs flour*
*1/2 cup cider vinegar*
*1 tsp Better Than Bouillon™*
*Beef Base dissolved in*
*1 cup hot water*
*1/2 cup sugar*
*1/4 cup chopped onion*
*1/4 cup chopped celery*

Cook potatoes in Better Than Bouillon™ Beef Broth 30 minutes, or until tender. Let cool; peel and slice. Place sliced potatoes in a serving bowl.

In a large skillet, fry bacon until crisp. Remove from heat. Remove bacon with a slotted spoon and drain on paper towels. Crumble bacon; add to potatoes.

Drain off all but one Tbs bacon grease. Stir flour into bacon grease in skillet. Gradually add vinegar and Better Than Bouillon™ Beef Broth, stirring constantly to make a smooth mixture. Add sugar, onion and celery. Cook until sauce is hot and slightly thickened.

Pour hot sauce over potatoes and bacon; toss gently to coat. Serve hot.

# NEW POTATO SALAD
**Superior Touch**

*Use Vegetable Base*
*Servings: 8–10*

2 lbs new potatoes, cooked
    and quartered (leave
    unpeeled)
1/4 cup red wine vinegar
1/8 cup extra-virgin olive oil
1/4 tsp freshly ground black
    pepper
1/2 tsp Better Than
    Bouillon™ Vegetable
    Base
1/4 cup finely chopped red
    onion
1/2 cup finely chopped celery
1/4 cup chopped fresh
    parsley
1 1/4 cups mayonnaise
1/8 cup Dijon-style mustard
3 hard-cooked eggs, peeled
    and sliced thin

Place potatoes in large mixing bowl. While potatoes are still warm, sprinkle them with vinegar and olive oil. Add pepper, Better Than Bouillon™ Vegetable Base, red onion, celery, parsley, mayonnaise, and mustard. Mix well. Add about half of the sliced hard-cooked eggs; mix gently. Use remaining sliced eggs as garnish. Let the salad cool, then cover and refrigerate for a few hours or overnight.

# APPLE-CHEESE COLESLAW
**Tracy Blahut**

*Use Vegetable Base*
*Servings: 4*

1/4 cup sour cream
2 Tbs mayonnaise
1 tsp Better Than Bouillon™
    Vegetable Base
1/4 medium head green or
    red cabbage, finely
    shredded
1 tart apple, chopped
1/4 cup crumbled blue
    cheese

Mix sour cream, mayonnaise and Better Than Bouillon™ Vegetable Base; cover and refrigerate at least one hour. Toss mixture with cabbage and apple. Serve with blue cheese sprinkled on top.

# IDAHO POTATO SALAD
**Sarah Coleman**

*Use Chili Base*
*Servings: 6-8*

*4-6 medium or large Idaho potatoes, peeled and quartered*
*3 hard-cooked eggs, peeled, divided*
*1 medium onion, finely chopped*
*2-3 ribs celery, finely chopped*
*3 slices bacon, cooked crisp and crumbled*
*4 sweet pickle slices, chopped*
*1 1/2 teaspoons lime or lemon juice*
*1/2 tsp Better Than Bouillon™ Chili Base*
*2 tsp prepared mustard*
*1/4 tsp garlic powder*
*1-1 1/2 cups mayonnaise*
*1/2 tsp paprika*

Boil potatoes in water to cover 20 minutes, or until fork tender. Drain and let cool. Dice potatoes.

Put diced potatoes in large serving bowl. Chop 2 of the eggs; add to potatoes in bowl. Stir in remaining ingredients except the paprika. Mix well.

Slice the remaining egg; place slices around the edge of the bowl. Lightly sprinkle paprika on top. Refrigerate, covered, until ready to serve.

# CUCUMBER CLAM SALAD
**Patricia Michaels**

*Use Vegetable Base*
*Servings: 4-6*

*2-3 medium cucumber, peeled*
*1 6 1/2-oz can chopped clams, rinsed and drained*
*2 tsp Better Than Bouillon™ Vegetable Base*
*3/4 cup white vinegar*
*2 Tbs sugar*
*1/4 tsp pepper*
*Salt, to taste*

Cut cucumber in half lengthwise and remove seeds. Slice cucumber paper thin.

Mix clams, Better Than Bouillon™ Vegetable Base, vinegar, sugar, pepper, and salt, to taste.

Toss cucumbers with clam mixture. Cover and refrigerate at least 4 hours.

# DUTCH POTATO SALAD

**Superior Touch**

*Use Vegetable Base*
*Servings: 10–12*

1/4 cup sugar
1 Tbs plus 1 1/2 tsp flour
2 tsp Better Than Bouillon™
  Vegetable Base dissolved
  in 3/4 cup hot water
1/4 cup cider vinegar
2 Tbs bacon drippings or
  melted butter or mar-
  garine
1 egg, lightly beaten
2 tsp prepared mustard
2 Tbs mayonnaise
4 lbs potatoes, cooked,
  peeled and thickly sliced
4 hard-cooked eggs, peeled
  and coarsely chopped
8 slices bacon, cooked crisp
  and crumbled

In a small saucepan, combine sugar and flour. In a bowl, combine Better Than Bouillon™ Vegetable Broth, vinegar and bacon drippings; stir into sugar mixture. Stir in lightly beaten egg and mustard. Cook over medium-low heat, stirring constantly, until thickened. Remove from heat and let cool to lukewarm. Stir in mayonnaise.

In a large mixing bowl, combine potato slices, eggs, and bacon. Add dressing while it is still warm; toss gently to coat. Cover and refrigerate several hours before serving.

Serve chilled or warm. To serve warm, briefly reheat salad in a 350° oven or in a microwave oven.

# SPINACH-APPLE-BACON TOSS

**Stephanie Michaels**

*Use Vegetable Base*
*Servings: 6*

8 oz spinach, torn into bite-
  sized pieces
4 slices bacon, crisply fried
  and crumbled
1 red apple, cored and sliced
1/2 tsp Better Than
  Bouillon™ Vegetable
  Base
1/3 cup mayonnaise
3 Tbs orange juice
  concentrate

Toss spinach, bacon and apple together in a serving bowl. Mix Better Than Bouillon™ Vegetable Base, mayonnaise, and orange juice concentrate in a separate bowl.

Toss salad and dressing together just before serving.

# MULTI-COLORED PASTA SALAD
**Superior Touch**

*Use Vegetable Base*
*Servings: 6–8*

*4 cups cooked multi-colored*
*spiral pasta, rinsed in*
*cold water and drained*
*1/4 tsp Better Than*
*Bouillon™ Vegetable*
*Base dissolved in*
*1/4 cup hot water*
*1 cup sliced green onions*
*2 cups diced tomatoes*
*1 4-oz can chopped green*
*chilies, drained*
*1/2 cup sliced black olives*
*1 cup corn kernels*
*2 Tbs chopped fresh cilantro*
*2 Tbs lime juice*
*2/3 cup bottled medium-hot*
*picante sauce or salsa*
*Mayonnaise*

In large salad bowl, combine all ingredients except mayonnaise. Stir to blend well. Add enough mayonnaise to coat salad ingredients well. Refrigerate to let flavors blend before serving.

# WARM TURKEY AND PASTA SALAD
**Mel Klein**

*Use Vegetable Base*
*Servings: 6*

*3 Tbs Better Than Bouillon™*
*Vegetable Base dissolved*
*in 3 qts boiling water*
*1 8-oz pkg rainbow rotini*
*1 Tbs extra-virgin olive oil*
*1 tsp Better Than Bouillon™*
*Vegetable Base*
*2 small carrots, thinly sliced*
*2 small zucchini, thinly sliced*
*2 green onions, thinly sliced*
*1 1/2 cups chopped cooked*
*turkey*
*1/4 cup grated parmesan*
*cheese*
*1 1/2 cups bottled Italian*
*dressing*
*Freshly ground pepper*

Cook rotini in Better Than Bouillon™ Vegetable Broth according to package directions. Drain and set aside. Sauté vegetables in oil and Better Than Bouillon™ Vegetable Base until crisp-tender. In a large bowl, combine pasta, vegetables, turkey, cheese, and dressing; toss to mix well. Sprinkle with pepper. Cherry tomatoes and parsley sprigs may be used for a colorful garnish.

# PASTA SALAD
**Chef Jorge Bruce**

*Use Vegetable Base*
*Servings: 6*

1 8-oz pkg macaroni
1 Tbs vegetable oil
1 tsp Better Than Bouillon™
  Vegetable Base
1 6-oz jar marinated artichoke hearts
1/2 cup Italian salad dressing
2 Tbs cider vinegar
1 cup mayonnaise
1 tsp Better Than Bouillon™
  Vegetable Base
Black pepper, to taste
1/2 cup cooked broccoli
  flowerettes
1/2 cup peas
1/2 cup sliced black olives
1 cup cubed fresh tomatoes

Cook pasta according to package directions, adding oil and one tsp Better Than Bouillon™ Vegetable Base to cooking water. Drain well.

Place drained pasta in a large mixing bowl. Drain marinade from artichokes, pouring marinade over pasta. Add Italian salad dressing to pasta. Cut artichoke hearts into quarters; add to pasta. Gently mix.

In a small bowl, combine vinegar, mayonnaise, and Better Than Bouillon™ Vegetable Base. Season to taste with pepper. Pour over pasta mixture. Gently stir in broccoli, peas, olives, and tomatoes. Refrigerate overnight to let flavors blend. Mix gently before serving.

# SPICY REFRIED BEANS
**Jim Williams**

*Use Chili Base*
*Servings: 4–6*

1 1/2 tsp vegetable oil
1 4-oz can diced green
  chilies
2 Tbs Better Than Bouillon™
  Chili Base
1 medium onion, diced
1/2 tsp garlic powder
1/2 tsp oregano
1 large can refried beans

Heat vegetable oil in skillet and add chilies, Better Than Bouillon™ Chili Base, onion, garlic powder, and oregano. Stir in beans, heat, and serve.

# ETHEL'S EGGPLANT
**Joan Tanney**

*Use Vegetable Base*
*Servings: 6*

*1 Tbs olive oil*
*2 large onions, sliced*
*1 large green or red bell pepper, sliced*
*8 oz fresh mushrooms*
*6 Roma tomatoes or 1 28-oz can whole peeled tomatoes, drained*
*2 medium or 1 very large eggplant (peeled or unpeeled), cut into 3/4-inch slices*
*2 Tbs butter*
*2 Tbs flour*
*1 tsp Better Than Bouillon™ Vegetable Base dissolved in 1 cup hot water*
*2 1/2 Tbs dark soy sauce*
*1 cup grated sharp cheddar cheese*
*Grated parmesan cheese*

Preheat oven to 350°. Sauté onions, pepper, and mushrooms in olive oil over high heat for 7-8 minutes. Do not brown. Add tomatoes and cook 5 minutes. Sauté eggplant briefly over high heat and set aside. Over low heat, melt butter in small pan and beat in flour with whisk. Add one cup Better Than Bouillon™ Vegetable Broth and heat until thickened and smooth. Bring to a boil and remove from heat.

In oven-proof casserole, layer eggplant with onion mixture. To creamy vegetable liquid add the soy sauce and grated cheese. Heat and stir until cheese is melted and mixture is smooth. Pour sauce over layered vegetables, sprinkle with parmesan cheese, and bake uncovered for 35 minutes.

## LORENE'S LIGHT AND QUICK VEGETARIAN

*Use Vegetable Base*
*Servings: 4*

**Lorene Scalora**

1 1/2 Tbs Better Than Bouillon™ Vegetable Base dissolved in 2 cups hot water
3 Tbs extra virgin olive oil
9 large cloves garlic, minced
1 large white onion, cut in thin wedges
1 lb small mushrooms, sliced
5 medium carrots, sliced at an oval slant
1 14-oz carton firm tofu, drained and diced
1 large bunch fresh broccoli flowerettes
Salt and pepper, to taste

Heat Better Than Bouillon™ Vegetable Broth in saucepan over low heat. Sauté garlic, onion and mushrooms in olive oil in large skillet over medium heat until onion is clear. Add carrots and tofu. Pour in Better Than Bouillon™ Vegetable Broth, reduce heat, and cover. Cook for 20 minutes. Add broccoli flowerettes and salt and pepper, to taste. Cook an additional 10 minutes until broccoli is bright green and firm. Serve over rice or pasta (recipe page vii).

## PARSLEYED NEW POTATOES

**Lorayn M. Pinochi**

*Use Chicken Base*
*Servings: 8*

8 red potatoes
1 tsp Better Than Bouillon™ Chicken Base
2-3 tsp Better Than Bouillon™ Chicken Base dissolved in
3/4 cup boiling water
1/4 cup minced green onions
1/4 cup minced parsley
Pepper, to taste

In large saucepan, cover unpeeled potatoes in water. Bring to a boil and add Better Than Bouillon™ Chicken Base. Cover and simmer for 15 minutes.

Drain potatoes and, while still hot, peel and dice potatoes into 3/4 inch pieces. Gently toss with 3/4 cup Better Than Bouillon™ Chicken Broth. Mix well.

Add green onions and pepper. Marinate at least 3 hours. Reheat and toss with parsley.

# CARROT-STUFFED PATTY PAN SQUASH

*Use Chicken or Vegetable Base*
*Servings: 6*

**Peggie Atrat**

6 small (3–4-inch) patty pan
  squash
2 Tbs butter
1 cup diced onions
1/2 cup minced fresh parsley
3 cups grated carrots
2 cloves garlic, minced
1 tsp Better Than Bouillon™
  Chicken or Vegetable
  Base dissolved in
  1/2 cup hot water
3/4 tsp fresh thyme or 1/4
  teaspoon dried thyme
1/4 tsp ground rosemary
4 oz cream cheese, cut into
  cubes
1 tsp lemon juice
Pepper, to taste
Plain yogurt
Chopped green onions

Preheat oven to 350°. Blanch whole squash in boiling water for 5-8 minutes, or until just tender. Drain and plunge into cold water to stop squash from cooking further. Drain again and cut off stem end of squash. Scoop out and discard a small amount of the pulp.

Sauté onion in butter for 2 minutes. Add parsley, carrots, garlic, and Better Than Bouillon™ Chicken or Vegetable Broth. Cook, stirring constantly, until water evaporates. Add herbs, cream cheese, and lemon juice. Heat until the cheese melts. Season to taste with pepper. Place squash on baking sheet and spoon filling into squash. Bake for 15–20 minutes or until heated through. Serve with plain yogurt and chopped green onions.

# GARLIC MASHED POTATOES

**Lori Cooper**

*Use Chicken Base*
*Servings: 8*

2 Tbs olive oil
5 cloves garlic, crushed
4 lb red potatoes, partially
  peeled
1 tsp Better Than Bouillon™
  Chicken Base
1 8-oz package cream cheese
1 tsp Better Than Bouillon™
  Chicken Base dissolved
  in 1 cup hot water
Salt, to taste
Pepper, to taste
Fresh parsley sprigs

Sauté garlic in olive oil in a small saucepan over medium heat for 3-4 minutes. Do not let garlic brown; it should be soft and golden.

Cut potatoes into 2-inch pieces and place in large pot of boiling water with one tsp Better Than Bouillon™ Chicken Base. Boil gently for 40 minutes, or until potatoes mash easily with a fork. Drain potatoes and place in large mixing bowl. Add garlic and cream cheese while mashing potatoes by hand or with an electric mixer. Add Better Than Bouillon™ Chicken Broth, using enough to create a creamy texture. Season to taste with salt and pepper and garnish with parsley.

# BETTER THAN BEANS

**John Weeks**

*Use Beef Base*
*Servings: 6-8*

1 16-oz package Great
  Northern beans
8 cups water
1 Tbs Better Than Bouillon™
  Beef Base
1 large carrot, diced
1 rib celery, diced
1 large onion, chopped
1 turnip, diced
1 medium zucchini, diced
1 Tbs seasoned salt
8 oz low-fat kielbasa

Soak beans overnight. Drain beans and add 8 cups water, Better Than Bouillon™ Beef Base, vegetables, and seasoned salt. Cook for two hours on medium heat, or until beans are tender. Slice kielbasa thin and add to beans. Cook for 10 minutes, or until warm. Serve with garlic bread.

# BETTER SPINACH PIES
Joan Bredekamp

*Use Chicken Base*
*Yield: 24*

## FILLING

1 Tbs butter
1 tsp minced garlic
1 medium onion, chopped
1 red bell pepper, chopped
2 cups chopped fresh spinach
1 Tbs Better Than Bouillon™
   Chicken Base
1/4 cup grated Swiss cheese

## PASTRY

1 1/2 cups flour
1/4 cup finely snipped
   sun-dried tomatoes
1/2 cup unsalted butter
1 egg
1 Tbs Better Than Bouillon™
   Chicken Base
3 Tbs heavy cream

1 egg
1 Tbs milk

In a 10-inch pan, sauté garlic in butter for one minute. Add onion, red bell pepper, spinach, and Better Than Bouillon™ Chicken Base. Cover and cook on high for 4 minutes. Drain mixture to remove liquid. Place in small bowl and add cheese. Combine with spinach mixture. Season, if needed. Let cool.

*Pastry:* Blend flour and dried tomatoes in food processor. Cut butter into 10 pieces and place on top of flour. Process until butter is in small crumbs. Beat egg, Better Than Bouillon™ Chicken Base, and cream. Add to butter mixture while food processor is on. As soon as dough forms a ball away from the sides of the bowl, stop food processor and remove pastry. Place on a piece of plastic wrap and form into a ball. Cover and refrigerate one hour.

Cut pastry dough in half. On a lightly floured surface, roll out half of the dough to a 9x12-inch rectangle. Cut into 12 3-inch squares. Place about one tsp of spinach filling in center of each square and fold into a triangle. Press edges together with a fork. Place on ungreased baking sheet and make two diagonal slits in each turnover with a knife. Mix egg and milk and brush mixture over turnovers. Bake in 400° oven for 8–12 minutes.

# PUERTO RICAN STEWED SMALL RED BEANS

*Use Beef Base*
*Servings: 4–6*

(Habichuelas Rosadas Secas)

Chef Jorge Bruce

## B E A N S

1 lb dried small red beans
2 qt water (for soaking)
2 qt water (for boiling)
1 large russet potato, peeled
    and cubed

## S O F R I T O

(Stew Flavoring)

1 Tbs vegetable oil
1 oz salt pork, diced
1 oz lean cured ham, diced
1 green pepper, chopped
2 sweet chili peppers, peeled
    and chopped
1 onion, chopped
2 cloves garlic, chopped
10 fresh cilantro leaves
1/4 tsp dried oregano
1 tsp Better Than Bouillon™
    Beef Base

1/4 cup tomato sauce
2 1/3 tsp salt

Habenero hot sauce, to taste

To quickly rehydrate beans, first boil 2 quarts of soaking water and beans for 2 minutes. Remove from heat and soak for one hour.

Discard soaking water and any floating beans or skins.

Bring 2 quarts of water, cut potatoes and beans to a boil. Cover and simmer over low to moderate heat for one hour, or until beans are almost tender.

As beans cook, prepare the sofrito in a small cast iron pot. Heat oil and rapidly brown salt pork and ham. Reduce heat to low and sauté peppers, onion, garlic, cilantro, oregano, and Better Than Bouillon™ Beef Base for 8–10 minutes, stirring occasionally.

When beans are tender, there should be about one inch of water covering the beans (if not, add water). Add the sofrito, tomato sauce, and salt, stir thoroughly, and simmer over moderate heat for about one hour. Be careful not to burn the beans. Sauce should not be too runny or too thick.

Beans are excellent over or with rice, tortas, surullitos, tostones, etc. For spicy beans, add habenero hot sauce to taste.

# ORIENTAL CABBAGE

**John Laury**

*Use Chicken Base*
*Servings: 4*

1 1/2 tsp Better Than
  Bouillon™ Chicken Base
  dissolved in 1 1/2 cups
  water
1 tsp rice vinegar
1 Tbs cream sherry
1 very large firm, green cabbage, cored and sliced
  into very thin slices (7-
  8 cups)
2 large yellow onions, peeled
  and thinly sliced into
  rings
2 tsp mild curry powder
1/4 tsp fresh ground black
  pepper
2 Tbs  Better Than Bouillon™
  Chicken Base

Heat Better Than Bouillon™ Chicken Broth in a 3-quart covered saucepan. Remove from stove, uncover, and add vinegar and sherry.

Layer cabbage and onions alternately in broth, sprinkling each layer lightly with curry powder. Add ground pepper. Cover and bring to a hard boil. Reduce heat to a simmer and cook 10 minutes. Uncover and stir thoroughly. Cover and simmer for an additional 20 minutes.

Recipe may be prepared to this point, removed from heat, and reheated as needed. To serve, heat thoroughly, drain, and serve as a vegetable side dish with roasted meats, fowl, barbecued meat, or fish.

# PLANTAIN TOSTONES
**Chef Jorge Bruce**

*Use Vegetable Base*
*Yield: about 30*

*3 green plantains*
*5 cups water*
*1 Tbs salt*
*1 Tbs Better Than Bouillon™*
*    Vegetable Base*
*Vegetable or canola oil for*
*    frying*

Peel plantains and cut into one-inch diagonal slices. Place in bowl with half of the water, salt, and Better Than Bouillon™ Vegetable Base. Soak for 10 minutes. Drain.

In deep skillet, fry the slices over medium heat, one layer at a time in just enough oil to cover plantains. Fry 7 minutes (or until tender), turning once. Do not overcook. Remove from pan and flatten with the palm of your hand to 1/4-inch thick.

Place flattened slices in remaining water, salt, and Better Than Bouillon™ Vegetable Base to soak briefly. Soak only as many as can be fried at a single time. Remove from water seasoned water and refry until golden, crispy brown. Drain on absorbent paper and serve warm with salt to taste.

# SMOTHERED OKRA
**Superior Touch**

*Use Chili Base*
*Servings: 10-12*

*7 8-oz bags frozen okra*
*1 small onion, chopped*
*2 Tbs oil*
*1 large can stewed tomatoes*
*1 8-oz bag frozen corn*
*1 Tbs seasoned salt*
*1 tsp lemon pepper*
*2 Tbs Better Than Bouillon™*
   *Chili Base*
*2 Tbs gumbo filé*
*1/2 lb smoked turkey*
   *sausage*
*1/2 lb large shrimp, shelled*
   *and deveined*

Sauté okra and onion in oil several minutes. Add tomatoes, corn, salt, pepper, Better Than Bouillon™ Chili Base, and filé and bring to a boil. Cover and simmer 20 minutes. Add sausage and shrimp and cook until shrimp just turn pink. Serve with rice (recipe page vii).

# CREAMED ONIONS
**Patricia Michaels**

*Use Vegetable Base*
*Servings: 4-6*

*1 1/2-2 lbs small white*
   *onions, peeled*
*3 tsp Better Than Bouillon™*
   *Vegetable Base dissolved*
   *in 4 cups hot water*
*2 Tbs butter*
*2 tsp Better Than Bouillon™*
   *Vegetable Base*
*2 Tbs flour*
*1/2 tsp pepper*
*1 1/2 cups half and half*
*1 1/2 cups shredded carrots*

Boil onions in Better Than Bouillon™ Vegetable Broth until tender, 15-20 minutes. Drain.

Heat butter and Better Than Bouillon™ Vegetable Base over low heat; whisk in flour and pepper. Cook until mixture is smooth and bubbly. Remove from heat and stir in half and half. Heat to boiling, stirring constantly. Boil and stir one minute. Stir in carrots and cook 5 minutes longer. Pour sauce over hot onions.

# POTATO AND TUNA SALAD

**Superior Touch**

*Use Vegetable Base*
*Servings: 6*

*1-1/2 lb piece fresh tuna*

*1-1/2 tsp Better Than
    Bouillon™ Vegetable
    Base dissolved in 1-1/2
    cups hot water*
*1/4 cup white wine*
*1 carrot, chopped*
*1/2 onion, chopped*
*1 celery rib, chopped*
*1/8 tsp pepper*

*3/4 lb potatoes*
*2 tsp Better Than Bouillon™
    Vegetable Base dissolved
    in 2 cups hot water*
*8 hard boiled eggs, quartered*
*3/4 lb tomatoes, thinly sliced*
*Dill Caper Sauce (recipe page
    162)*

Heat Better Than Bouillon™ Vegetable stock, wine, carrot, onion, celery and pepper to simmering. Carefully submerge tuna in simmering liquid and poach 15 minutes over low heat, covered.

Meanwhile, boil the potatoes in the Better Than Bouillon™ Vegetable stock until just tender. Peel and slice.

Remove poached tuna from heat. Flake tuna into bite-sized pieces. Place the flaked tuna and sliced potatoes in the poaching liquid to cool. When completely cooled, drain.

In a salad bowl, place tuna, potatoes, tomatoes and eggs and toss gently. Season with Dill Caper Sauce and serve.

# General Cooking Information

<table>
<tr><td colspan="2">ABBREVIATIONS</td></tr>
<tr><td>approx</td><td>approximately</td></tr>
<tr><td>doz</td><td>dozen</td></tr>
<tr><td>lb</td><td>pound</td></tr>
<tr><td>oz</td><td>ounce</td></tr>
<tr><td>pkg</td><td>package</td></tr>
<tr><td>qt</td><td>quart</td></tr>
<tr><td>Tbs</td><td>tablespoon</td></tr>
<tr><td>tsp</td><td>teaspoon</td></tr>
</table>

## EQUIVALENT MEASURES

| | | |
|---|---|---|
| 3 tsp | = | 1 Tbs |
| 4 Tbs | = | 1/4 cup |
| 5 1/3 Tbs | = | 1/3 cup |
| 16 Tbs | = | 1 cup |
| 2 cups | = | 1 pint |
| 4 cups (2 pints) | = | 1 qt |
| 4 qts (liquid) | = | 1 gallon |

## SPICE GUIDE

**Allspice** - a pea-sized fruit that grows in Mexico, Jamaica, Central and South America. It has a delicate flavor which resembles a blend of cloves, cinnamon and nutmeg. *Common Uses:* whole-pickles, meats, boiled fish, gravies; ground-puddings, relishes, fruit preserves, baking.

**Basil** - the dried leaves and stems of an herb grown in the US and North Mediterranean area. It has an aromatic, leafy flavor. *Common Uses:* flavoring tomato dishes and sauces, turtle soup, cooked peas, squash, snap beans; sprinkled over lamb and poultry.

**Bay Leaves** - the dried leaves of an evergreen grown in the eastern Mediterranean countries. It has a sweet, herbaceous floral spice note. *Common Uses:* for pickling, stews, for spicing sauces and soup; also for spicing a variety of meats and fish.

**Caraway** - the seed of a plant grown in the Netherlands. Its flavor combines the tastes of anise and dill. *Common Uses:* baking breads, often added to sauerkraut, noodles, cheese spreads; adds zest to french fried potatoes, liver, canned asparagus.

**Curry Powder** - a ground blend of ginger, turmeric, fengreek seed, as many as 16 to 20 spices. *Common Uses:* Indian curry recipes such as lamb, chicken and rice, eggs, vegetables.

157

**Dill** - the small, dark seed of the dill plant grown in India, having a clean, aromatic taste. *Common Uses:* a predominant seasoning in pickling recipes; also adds pleasing flavor to sauerkraut, potato salad, cooked macaroni, and fish.

**Marjoram** - an herb of the mint family, grown in France and Chile. It has a minty-sweet flavor. *Common Uses:* in beverages, jellies and to flavor soups, stews, fish, sauces; also excellent for sprinkling on lamb while roasting.

**Oregano** - the leaf of a safe bush grown in Italy, Greece and Mexico. *Common Uses:* excellent flavoring for any tomato dish, especially Italian specialities.

**Paprika** - a mild, sweet red pepper grown in Spain, Central Europe and the US. Slightly aromatic and prized for brilliant red color. *Common Uses:* a colorful garnish for pale foods, and for seasoning goulash and salad dressings.

**Rosemary** - an herb grown in France, Spain and Portugal. It has a sweet, fresh taste. *Common Uses:* in lamb and chicken dishes, soups, stews.

**Sage** - the leaf of a shrub grown in Greece, Yugoslavia and Albania. Its flavor is camphoraceous and minty. *Common Uses:* for meat and poultry stuffing, sausages, meat loaf, hamburgers, stews, and salads.

**Thyme** - the leaves and stems of a shrub grown in France and Spain. It has a strong, distinctive flavor. *Common Uses:* for poultry seasoning, in croquettes, fricassees and fish dishes; also tasty on fresh sliced tomatoes.

**Turmeric** - a root of the ginger family, grown in India, Haiti, Jamaica and Peru. It is a mild, ginger-pepper flavor. *Common Uses:* as a flavoring and coloring in prepared mustard and curries; also for meats, dressings, and salads.

# Index

# Index by BETTER THAN BOUILLON™ Product

# NOTES

# NOTES

# NOTES